Eventing

EVENTING
The Book of the Three-Day Event

Text by CAROLINE SILVER

Photographs by AKHTAR HUSSEIN
Adviser LUCINDA PRIOR-PALMER

St. Martin's Press

New York

St. Martin's Press, Inc. 175 Fifth Ave., New York, N.Y. 10010
Printed in Great Britain
Library of Congress Catalog Card Number: 76-28058
First published in the United States of America in 1977
ISBN 0 312 27090 9

Acknowledgments

Thanks are due to help and encouragement from a great many people:
to Rachel Bayliss, Mary Gordon-Watson, MBE, Susan Hatherly, Janet Hodgson, Richard Meade and Captain Mark Phillips for generously giving up their time to comment on photographic sequences;
to Joanna Capjohn, Bruce and Carol Davidson, Simone French of the British Horse Society, Lieutenant-Colonel Frank Weldon and Barbara Kemp for tirelessly and good-humouredly answering an abundance of questions and for volunteering invaluable advice;
to Michael Moffett, who lucidly and amusingly provided all the material for the opening chapter, and to his parents, Mr and Mrs A.J. Moffett, who entertained a score of comparative strangers at their home for a slide showing of the photographic sequences;
to Major-General G.E. and Lady Doreen Prior-Palmer, who encouraged, instructed and sustained Caroline Silver through many months of insecurity and doubt, and who, whenever Lucinda was away, worked on the manuscript as a priority despite their many other commitments;
to Margaret Fraser, who designed the book despite hold-ups in a tight time schedule which were not of her own making; to Janet Dawes, who typed the manuscript at a moment's notice; and to Jane Fincher, who made the black-and-white prints for Akhtar Hussein;
to Peter Clarke, Midge Keator and Willie Smith, who inspired and encouraged Akhtar throughout the three years of his work on the book;
to John Lovesey, Sports Editor of the *Sunday Times*, who gave Caroline many opportunities to attend events and who was understanding and helpful when her book work and newspaper commitments conflicted; and to Michael Sissons of A.D. Peters & Company, who guided and stage-managed us all.

Acknowledgment is also due to a number of people who have contributed illustrations, namely Rowland B. Wilson, *Esquire*—p 19; Weiner, Menzendorf and Pelham Books—p 20; Radio Times Hulton Picture Library—p 23, nos 1–4; Sport and General (Press Agency) Ltd—p 29; J.H. Neill—pp 30–31; Carl Giles and *The Daily Express* (*London Express Service*)—p 33; Michael Gilmore—p 34; Ernst Werner—pp 36–37, 48, 50–51; Ed Lacey—pp 46–47; W.R. Hazzard Jr—pp 52–63; Findlay Davidson—p 67; Leslie Lane—p 97, no. 1. The line drawings are by Christine Bousfield, Ray Burrows and Corinne Clarke.

Contents

Acknowledgments   5

Foreword   9

A PERSONAL ACCOUNT
Rough Saturday   11

THE DEVELOPMENT OF EVENTING
Hardly a Man is Now Alive   18
A short history of eventing

International Eventing in the Seventies   28
BADMINTON 1973 UK
Course-building—an exceptionally demanding course
KIEV 1973 USSR
Strangers in a strange land – significance of one
particularly difficult fence – individual heroism for
the sake of the team
BURGHLEY 1974 UK
World Championships – new training methods publicly proven
LUHMUHLEN 1975 FDR
A challenge cloaked in elegance – problems of light and
shade – team spirit – the elements of chance
LEDYARD 1975 USA
The event as social occasion – the hand of fate
replayed

Bruce Davidson and the American Revolution   56
The pursuit of Interval Training in America and its
effect on international eventing

TRAINING AN EVENT HORSE
Starting from Scratch   64
Buying a young event prospect – problems of a green horse –
early schooling – the first season – whether to ditch a
novice – the second season; novice to intermediate events –
progress towards three-day event standard

Interval Training for a Three-Day Event   72
Planning a programme – physical training for the rider –
feeding the horse – the programme that won the 1975
European Individual Gold Medal

IN ACTION

At Any Event   79

> General approach to the one-day event – the three-day event:
> relaxing the horse on first arrival – briefing of competitors –
> walking the course – exercising the horse during the event –
> preparing for the dressage test – preparing for the speed and
> endurance test – relaxing the horse after the cross-country –
> preparing for the veterinary inspection – procedure during the
> veterinary inspection – walking the show jumping course –
> riding the horse in for show jumping – treatment after the
> show jumping – arrival home

Dressage   101

Roads and Tracks; Steeplechase   107

The Cross-Country: 110

> Work in the Box, penalties on the course

Show Jumping   141

THE MONTREAL OLYMPICS   145

Appendices   170

> Whether to event – type of horse to buy – early groundwork –
> training and feed notes for three-day eventing – physical
> exercise for the rider – equipment for horse and rider –
> entering an event – one-day event routine – treatment of
> horse on arrival home

Glossary   174

Index   176

Dedication

In memory of Lieutenant-Colonel R. B. 'Babe' Moseley,
who inspired and guided so many event riders,
in particular the young

Foreword

My fascination with eventing began when a total stranger, Lady Hugh Russell, allowed me to hang on to the back of her wildly overcrowded jeep for a drive round the 1975 European Championships cross-country course. During this two-hour inspection, though I am sure she will not now remember it, Lady Hugh generously and patiently explained to me some of the hazards of eventing and in particular the problems posed by the Luhmühlen course.

Because of her explanation I watched the following day's cross-country performance as if I were looking through binoculars at a landscape previously seen only through misted glass. A further dimension of pleasure was added because for the first time I identified with a competitor: not someone I knew personally, but a good friend of a good friend – Lucinda Prior-Palmer. When Lucinda subsequently won, I experienced at once a jolt of vicarious satisfaction and the beginnings of an understanding of what she had been doing.

The book was Akhtar Hussein's idea. When I met him a month after Luhmühlen he had already spent two years compiling a series of photographs of riders jumping fences, shot at nine frames a second so that what had happened was recorded in immense detail. For a reason that is still not clear to me he asked if I would write a text to his extraordinary photographs, and for a reason that must be clear to everyone I asked Lucinda if she would act as a source of information, as a general adviser, and as a check on everything that was written.

Our opening chapter is intended to give some idea of what it can feel like to ride in a three-day event. Following the development of eventing into the increasingly-popular sport that it is today, we felt that the training sections of the book should assume basic riding knowledge on the part of the reader, since anyone intending to take up eventing would probably have been riding for several years. Coming towards the end of the book, we hope that the reader will have acquired enough information to assess the finer points of the cross-country photographic sequences.

From what I have learned from Akhtar and Lucinda and from the many others who have generously given advice I am now able to walk a three-day event course with a reasonable degree of knowledge and a great deal of enjoyment. Through this book I hope that others who watch eventing may acquire a greater understanding of and pleasure from their sport, that people who hope to take up eventing will learn something of what lies ahead of them, and that even established event riders may find points of interest in the training methods and comments of some of the finest riders in the world.

Crooked Soley, Wiltshire   August 1976

A PERSONAL ACCOUNT

Rough Saturday

Around 5 o'clock Michael Moffett came in from the fields, his face warm with work, stung into colour by the sharp north wind. He had been siding up a hedge on his father's farm, getting the office out of his system with each sweep of the hook through the straggling thorn shoots of early spring. Four days earlier he had left the industrial fog of Birmingham to spend a long weekend exercising his twelve-year-old gelding, Demerara, pulling the bits of the horse's mane and tail that had not been thinned quite as fine as he liked and strapping the healthy coat to tone the muscles up, his own as well as his horse's. In the small stableyard behind the Queen Anne farmhouse Demerara, a good eater, had his face in his evening feed; the most Michael could see over the stable door was a large, muscular brown backside bulging under the horse blankets and a shining, perfectly-pulled black tail.

It was Tuesday, 10 April, 1973, the night before Badminton Horse Trials, oldest and most famous of the British three-day event courses and a favourite of Michael's. He had first competed there on Demerara in 1970 and had enjoyed it so much that he had now arranged his annual week of holiday from his training in chartered accountancy to coincide with the event.

In the tack room Jill, Michael's groom, was packing up the horse-clothing for the trip, emptying most of the room into a trunk: it is difficult to forecast how many spares of rugs, towels, bandages, overreach boots, scrapers, studs and so on may be needed if anything gets wet or lost or broken. Michael, who had been a serious and successful competitor since 1966, knew from experience that it was safer to take everything. He closed the trunk and carted it outside into the horse trailer, adding feed and hay to the load so that Demerara would have his usual diet throughout the coming test.

Afterwards, in the farmhouse, before and after supper with his parents, his sister Sarah and younger brother Stephen, Michael worked on his boots and spurs, polishing over and over until the high, soft gleam of the leather and the sparkle of metal were fine enough to pass a cavalry inspection. He cleaned up the silk top hat he would wear for the dressage test, packed a couple of pairs of breeches, a sweater for the cross-country, his dressage tails, show

Michael Moffett and
Demerara, Badminton 76.

jumping coat, socks, underwear, dark suit for the traditional Thursday evening cocktail party, black tie for the Saturday night dance, and added a couple of hunting shirts to wear underneath anything and everything in case the weather was cold.

He went to bed early and happy, and got up conscious that there was nothing left to do but bandage up the horse and load him into the trailer. Nonetheless he did a routine double check on the equipment stacked in the left-hand partition of the trailer, making sure he had the saddle and bridle in – he would feel rather stupid if he hadn't – and that his mother had remembered the Wellington boots which are advisable if you mean to test the depth of the lake at Badminton. Loading Demerara was quick and easy, as the horse was an excellent traveller. Michael closed up the back of the trailer, said goodbye to his family (also event enthusiasts, they would join him later in the day), and got into the Land Rover with Jill. By eight o'clock they were on the road.

At Badminton Demerara had been assigned a loosebox for his five-day stay. He was a bold, calm sort, best left to settle into his strange surroundings by himself, so Michael simply shut the door on him and cut off down the road to the village hall, where most of the half-hundred or so other competitors were already jostling through the lobby, picking up their course plans in readiness for the 10 a.m. briefing by Lieutenant-Colonel Frank Weldon, the Director of Badminton, who would explain the rules of the event. Some came with parents, wives, or husbands, nodding to friendly rivals, laughing over-easily at Colonel Weldon's dry humour, getting on each other's nerves in the rising tension. Michael preferred to be on his own.

When the briefing was over everyone climbed into Land Rovers for the ritual drive round the eight miles of roads and tracks that formed part of the coming Saturday's speed and endurance test. Since many of the competitors had ridden the same roads and tracks in other years, this part of the inspection of the course had become less an examination of the route than a contest in strategic driving, a rivalry for first place behind Weldon's leading vehicle along the woodland paths of the Badminton estate. Half-way round they disembarked to walk the two-mile steeplechase course. Finally, bursting out of the constricting trees into the open straights of Worcester Avenue, the two-mile front approach to the Duke of Beaufort's colossal country house, the mass of vehicles drew level, manoeuvring like stock cars to get behind their leader.

In front of Badminton House, beside the main arena and the trade stands, beer tents, press tents, officials', members' and competitors' tents, beside the car parks and the lake, the cross-country course began. This, the toughest test of the event, would be walked several times by each competitor. For the first inspection Michael liked to go along with the crowd, taking part in the cracks and backchat that covered up the nerves as each of the 35 formidable fences was inspected, not bothering at that stage to do much more than get a general sense of the four-and-a-half mile route.

After lunch he took Demerara up into Badminton Park for a quick run-through of the dressage test. He practised the movements in random order, careful to give Demerara's excellent but not perfect memory no basis for false assumption in the following morning's performance. Other horses and riders were scattered here and there across the parkland, most working intently on their dressage. Michael rode up through the tents and stands and got told off for leaving hoofprints in the public ground.

By 5 o'clock, having walked the cross-country and steeplechase courses again, he was back at Badminton Stables for the routine veterinary inspection of all competing horses that is held before every three-day event. Interested spectators – mostly other competitors, relatives, press, photographers and course officials – watched each horse walk up before the examiners, stand for scrutiny, trot away and back before the panel. Demerara felt keen, limber and fine-toned from his three months of hard training. He squealed and put in a buck on the turn to trot back. 'He doesn't look very different from last year,' one of the examiners, a local veterinary surgeon, said to Michael.

That night, in a hotel a few miles from the course, Michael read over the dressage test to refresh his memory. He had been drawn early on in the two days needed for all the competitors to complete the dressage phase, and knew it meant that Demerara was not highly regarded as a dressage horse since all the best performers were assigned to Friday afternoon, when Badminton would be televised. It did not signify: the dressage test, like the show jumping, is relatively unimportant in three-day eventing. The cross-country, in which Demerara had put up the fastest time in four out of his last eight events, is the important part, the comparative scoring ratio being roughly, dressage 3 : cross-country 12 : show jumping 1.

Michael was woken at 6.30 with coffee and newspapers. He lay in bed for a few minutes laughing at the reports of the equestrian correspondents, some of which were forecasting a favourite that had been withdrawn from Badminton two weeks before.

An hour and a half before his test he began to ride Demerara in, working with a deep seat to supple the horse and collect him up into his bridle until Demerara flowed with a fluid grace over the turf, neck arched proud and toes pointed delicately into each stride. Then, top-hatted and tail-coated, Michael rode into the dressage arena and picked up 74 penalty points for the ten-minute test, which was to put him about two-thirds down the list at the end of the first day. A bit better than he had expected. He was happy: he stretched Demerara out for a canter after the dressage and the horse felt marvellously well.

That evening, with less than two days to go before the great test of speed and endurance, a horse two doors along from Demerara was heard to cough. It was a worrying moment for everyone with horses in the same stable block, as the cough is highly infectious. Shortly afterwards the cougher was boxed up and sent home.

On Friday, having taken Demerara for a short pipe-opener to clear his wind and been reassured to find that the horse still felt happy and well, Michael walked the cross-country course again. He went by himself, trying to avoid contact with other competitors or trainers because he was afraid that with so many experts on the course he might start listening to them, which he knew could be disastrous. He felt that if he did not see a problem it tended not to exist for him.

He tried to visualise the course as it would look next day, when the mass of spectators would alter the perspective on each fence and the course ropes would bulge inwards under the weight of the people, leaving not as much room to turn as the rider had come to expect. He grinned to himself – Demerara was always a horse to hang on to the ropes, and he had found that when he cut a corner tightly baby carriages and photographers disappeared like speeded-up film. Photographers in particular were apt to stand their ground until the last second, and Demerara had had a couple of them in the past.

Though the course alters from year to year the Badminton fences are always big and problematical. Coming as it does in the spring, the event serves as a proving ground for British aspirants to whatever international championship – European, World or Olympic – is due to follow in the summer. Walking the first half of the course before lunch, Michael spent extra time at the eighteenth fence, a 3′ 6″-high stone wall obscuring a dropped landing into rising ground. Studying it from all angles he could see no way to jump it that would avoid smacking into the far side of the gully; in fact, the better he might jump it the harder the jar on landing, since the gully was too wide to be cleared by the speed of the horse's flight. The secret of riding a cross-country course lay in keeping the horse flowing steadily along, maintaining a rhythm from start to finish; yet at this wall he saw no way around being stopped by the landing and having to pick the horse up and start all over again.

He came to the lake, fence number 20 of the 35, and felt happier. Many horses would be unbalanced by the drag of the water on the landing side of the three-foot high woodpile, but Demerara's powerful body could dive through this sort of problem like a hungry duck.

Since the Badminton course lay-out is roughly a figure of eight, Michael was now back at the centre of action. He stopped off for a salad in the members' tent, and watched the dressage for a while before walking the rest of the course.

During the evening he chewed over his approach to the course, thinking not so much about specific approaches to each fence – by now he had worked out his basic strategy for each – but about the course as a whole, trying to gauge how much energy would be absorbed by the unusually difficult problems posed by this tough but jumpable course, and when it would be safe to start putting on the pressure.

The big day, the high point of Michael's holiday, came in overcast and warm. Opening the box door on Demerara, he knew at once that something was wrong. The horse had a staring coat and had not eaten up. The loss of appetite was not in itself a great worry, because Demerara often left his feed at Badminton; probably, Michael guessed, because of the exciting voices of the Duke of Beaufort's foxhounds, which were kennelled within earshot of the horses. Since Demerara looked neither happy nor right Michael took his temperature, something he had seldom needed to do during the eight years of his association with this basically very healthy horse, and was surprised to find that it was normal. He asked his father for advice. Mr Moffett, a surgeon and the son of a veterinary surgeon, examined the horse very carefully but could find nothing wrong.

Michael hung around the stable yard unhappily, the minutes ticking by too fast towards the moment of decision on whether or not to withdraw his entry. Not normally a worrier, he worried now about the things his instinct told him about his horse; yet, because they could find nothing wrong and because Demerara's temperature was perfect, reason insisted that he would be foolish not to run the horse. He fitted Demerara's tendon boots, asked Jill to lead the horse up to the starting point, and took his saddle to the scales to weigh out.

During phase A of the roads and tracks Michael's suspicions that something must be wrong were increased: to keep within the official time he had to canter most of the way. Normally Demerara would complete this part of the speed and endurance test at a trot; yet, again, there was nothing but the lack of speed to suggest that the horse was not moving along well within himself. The dilemma was substantiated in phase B, the steeplechase, when Demerara jumped accurately but so slowly that he incurred 22.4 time penalties. Normally Michael would expect to complete the course without any penalties.

Phase C of the roads and tracks seemed interminable, cantering all the way to keep within the time, turning at last into Worcester Avenue with the two-mile view to home and the horse now off the bit. The massed crowds around Badminton House seemed to draw no nearer with each sluggish step. Michael was glad that the course veterinary surgeons would watch him trot into the fenced-off paddock called the Box, where competitors took a ten-minute break before starting the cross-country, and where Demerara would be examined to see if he was fit to continue.

He hopped off the horse as he trotted in. The veterinary panel passed him fit. Relieved, though still uneasy, Michael quickly unsaddled so that his family and the groom could begin on the usual rush job of freshening Demerara up for the cross-country. First, towels were tied round the tops of his legs to keep excess water off the boots and bandages while Demerara's body was washed from head to tail and the surplus water scraped off by two girls with a third to hold the horse's head. Mrs Moffett moved in with towels to dry

Albrighton Woodland Pony Club one-day event, 1962. Michael and Tuppence.

the offside, while Jill rubbed the nearside down and sister Sarah dried the legs. Michael, who had been asking other competitors and officials how the course was riding, came back in time to check the boots and bandages and wash his horse's mouth out thoroughly with a spongeful of water. The horse was walked dry in a sweat rug, saddled up and mounted. Michael sharpened him up with a quick canter on the spot, then the count came down and they were away.

Demerara went off with a shorter stride than usual, lolloping rather than bounding along. He jumped the first and second fences well, and at the third, the Coffin (one of the most difficult jumps on the course – a post and rails on to a down-slope, over a ditch, up a bank over another post and rails) he jumped exceptionally well. Over the unsighting problem of the odd-shaped Diamonds, the trappy Zig Zag rails over an open ditch, in and out over the fences at Luckington Lane, and in and out handily over the right-angled Tom Smith's Walls the horse jumped steadily and carefully; so that coming into the Bullfinch, a tall, straggling thorn hedge designed to be jumped through, Michael felt free to concentrate on handling the sharp right turn beyond the hedge and leave the fence largely to his horse.

Demerara didn't go through the Bullfinch: he jumped *over* it, and in the huge attempt landed short, caught a leg in the ditch on the landing side and turned right over. Michael saw his horse coming over on top of him and rolled as fast as he could to get clear, but nevertheless one of Demerara's legs came down across the nerve on Michael's elbow and knocked all feeling out of his arm. A man whom he took to be the fence judge came out of the crowd and threw him back up in the saddle.

Michael had been winded by the fall and Demerara, though

Cotswold Vale Pony Club one-day event, 1966. Michael (16) with Demerara, then five years old.

unhurt, had lost confidence. For the next two fences they scrambled rather than jumped, Michael's useless arm an added hindrance. Crossing Luckington Lane for the second time Demerara ducked out at the second fence ... and then it all started to go right again. Over the Open Water and the post and rails and ditch of the Vicarage Vee, a superb jump at the Stockholm Fence, another over the Irish Bank, down with confidence to the Stone Wall ... and smack into the rise on the landing side, which ground Demerara to a standstill. Over the following Parallel Rails he went reasonably well, being a parallel specialist, but Michael could tell the horse had lost some of his nerve after the wall. He went into the Lake more gingerly than usual, floundered slightly on landing, and Michael, who still hadn't got his wind back properly from the fall at the Bullfinch, tipped off into the water.

'I remember the lake was incredibly warm, which I didn't expect at all,' he said afterwards. 'I got back up, but I realised I was now very insecure in the saddle one way or another, so I jumped back out of the lake and retired.'

Demerara was shipped back home that night. He had been incubating equine influenza, presumably caught from the cougher in the same stable block, but was fully recovered within a few days. The numbness in Michael's arm took six months to disappear completely, though it never caused him serious trouble.

In the week after Badminton Michael went ahead with preparations for his next three-day event. It might seem strange that after such a rough ride on Saturday he should want to do so, but to Michael, as to any event rider, what had happened was part of the game.

THE DEVELOPMENT OF EVENTING

Hardly a Man is now Alive

Listen, my children, and you shall hear,
Of the midnight ride of Paul Revere,
On the eighteenth of April, in Seventy-five;
Hardly a man is now alive
Who remembers that famous day and year.
  H. W. LONGFELLOW, *Paul Revere's Ride*

If Paul Revere's horse had refused to go, there would not have been any ride, and the American War of Independence might have had a different beginning. Equally, knights would have looked ungallant trying to carry off their ladies on chargers which were unsound, disobedient or stubborn. Unnumbered military messages would never have been delivered without fit, well-trained horses to bear them; for example, news of the Russian repulse during the Russo-Turkish war of 1878 was carried the 93 miles from Silistra to Varna in a short afternoon by the Arab stallion Omar Pasha (whose rider dropped dead of exhaustion on arrival, and so could not have been much help to the horse during the last few miles of the journey).

Behind the modern three-day event lie milennia of recognition of the values of speed, endurance, obedience and mobility in the horse. This recognition has been especially strong among military men, whose lives have so often depended on their horses' readiness to obey. More than two thousand years ago Xenophon ordered that cavalry horses should be kept well fed and fit, since 'a horse which cannot endure fatigue will clearly be unable to overhaul the foeman or effect escape;' further that horses should be thoroughly trained, as 'a horse that will not obey is only fighting for the enemy and not for his friends.' Xenophon seems also to have understood the essence of the horse as such, in contrast to much of today's misconceived anthropomorphism: 'If oxen and horses or lions had hands, and could paint with their hands, and produce works of art as men do, horses would paint the forms of gods like horses.'

Mohammed, another military genius, did more than anyone before or since to enforce upon his people a value for the horse above all

'The British are coming . . . uh . . . to my house . . . um . . . for Sunday dinner . . . be there . . . ' The Rowland B. Wilson cartoon first appeared in *Esquire* in 1962.

other possessions. So convinced was he of the military importance of the tough desert horses of north Africa, which he bought from nomadic tribes and paid for with human slaves, that he wrote into the Koran a number of commands that have enforced a Muslim reverence for the horse for more than thirteen centuries. Among them are an irresistible injunction to men to feed their horses well ('As many grains of barley as thou givest thy horse, so many sins shall be forgiven thee') and a nice one, aimed at the superstitious, to

The 1936 Olympic gold medallist, Capt L. Stubbendorf of West Germany, on Nurmi.

encourage selective breeding and the safekeeping of the product ('The Evil One dare not enter into a tent in which a pure-bred horse is kept').

The power that commandments of this sort had over the bedouin tribes is evident in legends such as the following:

'Allah said to the South Wind: "Become solid flesh, for I will make a new creature of thee, to the honour of My Holy Name, and the abasement of Mine enemies, and for a servant to them that are subject to Me."

'And the South Wind said: "Lord, do Thou so."

'Then Allah took a handful of the South Wind and he breathed thereon, creating the horse and saying: "Thy name shall be called Arabian, and virtue bound into the hair of thy forelock, and plunder on thy back. I have preferred thee above all other beasts of burden, inasmuch as I have made thy master thy friend. I have given thee the power of flight without wings, be it in onslaught or retreat. I will set men on thy back, that shall honour and praise Me and sing Hallelujah to My name."'

Mohammed does not seem to have attached any importance to the art of jumping. Nor indeed did anyone else up until the 'leaping contests' of the late nineteenth century, though mention is made of it in a seventeenth-century instruction to the Swedish cavalry ('When jumping a fence the rider will grab the mane, close his eyes, and shout "hey"'). This absence of emphasis on what would be a severe disadvantage in the horse of today was doubtless because very little land was enclosed until recent times.

But the importance of long-distance endurance tests which did not involve jumping has been appreciated by international cavalry for at least three centuries, notably in France, Germany, Sweden and the United States. In a growing international move to combine the skills of dressage and jumping with those of speed and endurance (hence 'combined training', a synonym for 'eventing'), it was France who, in 1902, first produced a contest similar to the modern three-day event. The *Championnat du Cheval d'Armes*, held in and around Paris and limited to military horses only, divided into four phases in the following order: dressage, steeplechase, 5km of roads and tracks, and show jumping.

Though combined training, or 'Military', as it was universally known for the first part of this century and as it is still called in Europe, quickly became popular throughout much of Europe it was not until 1912 that it – or *any* form of equestrian competition, come to that – was first included in the Olympic Games; and this inclusion was due to an almost singlehanded fight by Count Clarence von Rosen, Master of the Horse to the King of Sweden, who had been battling for six or seven years for Olympic recognition of equestrian sports.

Appropriately, the first Olympic three-day event was held in Stockholm, with Sweden carrying off both the team and individual trophies. As is again the case today (teams of three were the rule in the middle of this century), teams of four from any one nation competed, with the scores of only the best three counting towards the team championship. Ten nations took part, including the United States, Belgium and Great Britain, and Sweden, Germany and France ran off with nearly all the prizes in all of the equestrian competitions.

The results of the Olympic three-day events up until the Second World War give some idea of who was playing seriously and who was not. The 1916 Olympics, scheduled for Berlin, never got off the ground for obvious reasons, but here are the subsequent winners:

1920 Antwerp *Team*: 1. Sweden, 2. Italy, 3. Belgium.
      Individual: Count H. Mörner, Sweden.

1924 Paris   *Team*: 1. Holland, 2. Sweden, 3. Italy.
      Individual: Lt. A. v d V. van Zijp, Holland.

1928 Amsterdam *Team*: 1. Holland, 2. Norway, 3. Poland.
      Individual: Lt. Ch. Pahud de Mortanges, Holland.

1932 Los Angeles *Team*: 1. USA, 2. Holland. (No third team finished.)
      Individual: Lt. Ch. Pahud de Mortanges, Holland.

1936 Berlin   *Team*: 1. Germany, 2. Poland, 3. Great Britain.
      Individual: Capt. L. Stubbendorf, Germany.

The British, now one of the finest three-day event producers in the world, did not at first take the Military seriously. Apart from the Indian Army School of Equitation at Saugor (who organised colossal endurance tests consisting of a 60-mile ride in 24 hours, broken by an overnight bivouac on the banks of the River Bewas, but followed without a break by a ten-furlong gallop over eight big steeplechase fences, and then, after a half-hour check on the horses' condition, by a short but complicated *manège* – indoor – test), the atmosphere at Weedon in England was apathetic. Cavalry instructors at Weedon would order their pupils, 'You, you, and you will go to the Olympics,' only to be answered with excuses such as, 'Oh no, sir, I'm playing polo.' One Olympic enthusiast, appalled at the grass-fat softness of the British Olympic entries, commented sarcastically that the horses looked very well. He was met with the bright reply, 'Thank you, Sir. Yes, they'll be just about ready when the cubbing season starts.'

After the war the game was thrown open to civilians. The first postwar Olympics was held in London, where the team event went to the USA and the individual gold to Capt. B. Chevallier of France. Here, thanks largely to the interest displayed by the famous master of foxhounds, the Duke of Beaufort, who thereafter organised annual three-day events at his home, Badminton, Britain began to take up eventing seriously.

Olympic results following London show changes as more and more nations became interested and travel facilities got easier:

1952 Helsinki	*Team*: 1. Sweden, 2. Germany, 3. USA. *Individual*: Capt. H von Blixen-Finecke, Sweden.
1956 Melbourne	(Equestrian events held in Stockholm because of Australian quarantine laws) *Team*: 1. Great Britain, 2. Germany, 3. Canada. *Individual*: Sgt. P. Kastenman, Sweden.
1960 Rome	*Team*: 1. Australia, 2. Switzerland, 3. France. *Individual*: L. Morgan, Australia.
1964 Tokyo	*Team*: 1. Italy, 2. USA, 3. Germany. *Individual*: M. Checcoli, Italy.
1968 Mexico City	*Team*: 1. Great Britain, 2. USA, 3. Australia. *Individual*: Adj. J-J. Guyon, France.
1972 Munich	*Team*: 1. Great Britain, 2. USA, 3. Germany. *Individual*: R. Meade, Great Britain.

Three-day eventing has become progressively more sophisticated as enthusiasm attracts larger and larger numbers of men and women into competition, while hard work, dedication and rising standards are producing quality performances across the board.

The object of dressage as part of eventing is to demonstrate the harmonious development of the horse and its perfect understanding with its rider; though event horses are unlikely ever to rival pure dressage animals in this field, partly because the event horse, trained to the peak of fitness for the following day's speed and endurance test, is often too full of himself to perform with maximum calm and concentration. The show jumping phase, on the third day when the horse may be tired and stiff after the cross-country phase, is little more than an obedience test, a demonstration of the horse's fitness, suppleness and willingness to continue.

It is the cross-country phase that signifies most in the test of an event horse, showing his and his rider's physical and mental agility over four-and-a-half miles of difficult fences, following directly after nine miles of roads and tracks and more than two miles on a steeple-chase course.

Nevertheless, 'The object of a three-day event is, or was, military,' Lieutenant-Colonel Frank Weldon, one of the most successful of the postwar British competitors and now designer of the Badminton course, reminds us. 'If, after a week of war, you had an unsound horse you had the unspeakable discomfort of having to walk.'

Overleaf, four pages of Diana Thorne riding The Kingmaker over one of Weldon's fences, the Double Ski Jump at Badminton in 1976, show that the discomforts of having to walk may not nowadays be so unspeakable.

1. Judges watch the show jumping during the Badminton trials in 1949.

2. The days of rolled shirt-sleeves: a competitor during the cross-country at Warlingham in 1954.

3. Badminton in its early days. The horse slipped approaching the jump.

4. Badminton in 1952. Major Miller on Stella – at show jumping at least little has changed.

BADMINTON 1976
Double Ski Jump and Faggot Pile

Diana Thorne on The Kingmaker

2

4

Two drop fences on a downhill slope, with upward ramps before each element. Maximum height of second fence, the rails, three feet. The drops – the crux of the problem – were not visible to the horse until the last moment.

This was an excellent test of the rider's control and of the trust and courage of her horse. The difficulty lay in approaching with sufficient momentum to avoid a refusal, yet not so fast that the horse's speed would jar him with a punishing landing or that he would go out of control as he strode downhill away from each fence.

The combination started with a sharp left-hand swing into the first element (1, opposite), and led on to the option of a left- or right-hand jump over the 'v'-shaped second fence (this page). Choice of route was governed by yet a third fence, the Faggot Pile (overleaf), which required a right-hand turn into an uphill approach.

Diana Thorne and The Kingmaker, a very bold horse, took the shortest way through. On a horse with less courage the rider could be said to be sitting slightly too far forward throughout, but knowledge of her horse had taught her not to expect a refusal or a blunder on landing. Her problem was a possible loss of control. Note that she never slips her reins on landing, and that her contact with The Kingmaker's mouth remains constant all the way.

For comparison, see pages 120-3.

5

6

7

8

9

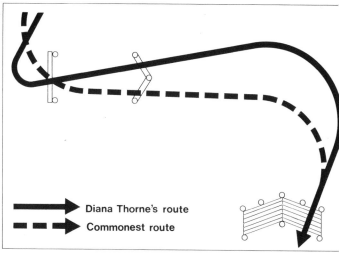

Diana Thorne's route
Commonest route

10

11

The sketch at the top of the page shows the route Diana Thorne took through the Double Ski Jump and the following Faggot Pile. Her course is marked in unbroken line. The dotted line is the route chosen by most of the other competitors.

Landing after the Double Ski Jump, the rider had to maintain control in order to make a tight turn back uphill over the Faggot Pile. A foot outside the pegged-out penalty zone would have cost 10 points.

Diana said it had been difficult for her to make the tight turn uphill for the Faggot Pile, as The Kingmaker takes a strong hold. 'I thought I might not make the turn for the log pile if I went the short way, but I chanced it.'

The chance took her through the combination in excellent time.

12

9. Leaving the Double Ski Jump behind, The Kingmaker wants to pull away down the hill. Note the balance and the power of the hind-quarters, which make the tight uphill turn (10) possible.

11, 12 and 13. He lengthens his stride on the uphill approach, meeting the fence powerfully.

14. A perfect jump over the 3′10″ fence which will carry him easily over the 4′6″ spread.

15. An almost flippant landing, as if the horse had been jumping over a small log.

16. Going away he still needs a tight rein. At this point he has completed 14 miles of the speed and endurance test.

International Eventing in the Seventies

The growth of public interest in eventing and the consequent involvement of more and more civilians as competitors are the natural outcome of two influences that were not available during the first half of this century: television coverage and air transport for horses. Like a whirlpool spiralling outwards, people from all nations have become increasingly able to understand the capabilities and scope of horses – as well as their limitations – and those who want to compete find it a little easier each year to get their horses to competition sites. (Competitors have also had to learn that, in international events, though they are ostensibly present for their horsemanship, there are other considerations, such as the social life of eventing and the fact that overseas they are also ambassadors for their country.)

While this in no way means that courses are becoming standardised, it does mean that national and international courses of recent years are uniformly improving in quality and safety all the time. In the early days of eventing, little was established about the endurance capacities of the horse and training was often at least inadequate if not inhumane by modern standards. In a mechanised society, the value of the horse in war gives place to its comparatively luxurious life as a plaything for human leisure, and so both logic and illogic exist in the argument that it is acceptable to sacrifice horses in the interest of killing humans, but unacceptable to injure horses in pursuit of human pleasure.

Criteria change with the times. Until the mid-fifties there were no standard rules governing three-day events. When international rules were first laid down, with limitations of height and spread, course builders were initially inclined to make *every* fence of maximum height and/or spread, with a consequently heavy casualty toll of horse and rider. Modern sophistication in course building has become comparatively lenient on horses while simultaneously ensuring a heavier psychological burden on the riders.

The following five courses, all famous and all international, illustrate some of the problems facing course-builders and competitors in the developing spirit of the nineteen-seventies.

Lt-Col Frank Weldon, now Badminton's course designer, competing on Kilbarry in front of Badminton House during the dressage phase in 1956. Later that year he captained the British Olympic team in Stockholm.

OVERLEAF: Lucinda Prior-Palmer and Be Fair at the Log Pile, Badminton 1973.

Badminton 1973 UK

'The art of designing a good course,' wrote Colonel Weldon in a preview to Badminton 1973 for the London *Daily Telegraph*, 'is to frighten the wits out of the riders on their feet, but not to hurt the horses on the day.' The cross-country he designed for that year was one of the toughest and most intimidating Badminton courses of all time, a strategic masterpiece that could be jumped only by a bold, quick-thinking rider on a bold, obedient horse.

The problems of Badminton 73 were essentially the normal problems posed by any great course:

The intricacies of combination fences involving more than one element to be jumped in any one obstacle;

The quantity of drop fences, which tend to break the forward rhythm of a horse and may cause him to lose heart;

The problems of optical delusion caused by building fences on a slant or other complicated pattern;

The problems of distance between fences. The obvious difficulties here lie in the number of strides between each element of a combination fence. The less obvious lie in maintaining rhythm and discipline over long stretches of open ground between fences, when most riders might think it safe to relax and in consequence have lost perfect control when eventually reaching the distant fence.

What made Badminton 73 so unusually harsh was the ingenious juxtaposition of these problems, and the relentless way in which, up until the final quarter of the course, they kept recurring. Of the first 28 fences 12 were drops, 13 were combinations, and several presented optical illusions which needed blind faith on the part of the horse. Since so many of the fences punished the horse with an unexpected drop or by landing into a bank, none but those who were totally obedient to and confident in their riders could hope to get round.

The most difficult fence, the Coffin, which eliminated a score of competitors, came unusually early on as fence number three, when horse and rider were still barely into their stride. What looked from the approach to be an in-and-out of posts and rails of reasonable heights (3′ 6″ and 3′ 9″) turned out to be a very tight landing over the first element on to a downslope, over a 4′-wide ditch on to rising ground, which increased the height of the final element unless the stride into the take off was very precisely judged. Thus, if the horse was coming in too fast he would not be able to shorten his stride quickly enough to get through without a fall, whereas if he came in slowly he would see the ditch at the last moment and would be likely to stop. What was needed was a short, bouncy stride into the fence, giving the horse sufficient time to register the ditch, get over the surprise, and have enough impulsion to go on.

"Lady, you don't happen to have one about horses being unfair to riders?"

The severity of the 1973 course provoked critics. This response appeared in the London *Daily Express*.

The second Luckington Lane crossing (12 and 13) offered another problem in ingenuity for which the horse could expect little reward. The approach over a 3′ 11″ wall left enough room for only one stride across the lane before the 3′ 9″ leap up on to the bank fronting the 3′ 2″ rails out over the drop – just enough room on top of the bank to land, but not enough to re-position or to check the forward momentum; so that unless the horse was perfectly placed on the bank the swing-up over the rails would result in a heavy thud into the drop.

The Stockholm Fence (16), based on a fence that caused a host of problems in the 1956 Olympics, was another punisher. The 3′ 9″ tree trunk suspended without a ground line in a gully offered possible problems in where to take off to clear it, and unavoidable problems in how to land without jarring the horse. Here, as in the next but one, the Stone Wall, the only landing answer could be bad: smack into the rising ground, with rhythm and momentum lost.

At the Lake (20 and 21) several riders fell into the water when the impact of landing over the first element stopped their horses short. The jump out up the railway-sleepered bank and rail, 3′ 11″ from the bottom of the water, was big, considering the inevitable slowness of the approach and the slight drag of the water on the horses' legs.

From the Lake a long stretch of open grassland gave plenty of time for horse and rider to be off the alert when coming downhill into the next, the formidable Normandy Bank. Here, a ditch fronted a jump on to the 3′6″ bank, the top too narrow for a restoring stride before the 3′7″-high rails in front opened into an eight-foot landing drop.

Another drop at the Ski Jump, though this could be taken slowly

Rachel Bayliss and Gurgle the Greek 'clear' the Stockholm fence. Following this incident it was ruled that horses must go *over* fences.

provided the horse would not stop when he saw the view, led on to the four elements of the Sunken Road – post and rails in, jump down into the road, jump up out of the road, and out over the 3′ 11″ wood-pile with a five-foot spread. Yet another combination, the Quarry (26 and 27), involved a drop and offered alternate routes. Either one had to negotiate two large sleepered steps downwards without a stride between, followed one stride away by a full-height stone wall; or one had to go over a 2′ palisade, the face an almost sheer ramp down into the bottom of a quarry, sharp left turn and over the same wall without going outside the penalty areas.

The last of the nasty questions for a tired horse and rider came seven fences from home: the Star, which could possibly be cleared by a single bound through the centre if sufficient strength and accuracy were left, or could be jumped through in two on a slant.

Badminton 1973 was not itself an international championship course, but a sorting ground to short-list the British team for the European Championships in Kiev. It was not a matter of sorting the sheep from the goats, since no goat in the world could have horned in there, but more one of finding the wolves in sheep's clothing. The winners were Lucinda Prior-Palmer and Be Fair. Be Fair received 53 congratulatory telegrams in the two days following the event.

Kiev 1973 USSR

The European Championships, held early in September, ran through a collective tomato farm and were originally planned to include half a mile of the Kiev–Odessa highway (use of the highway, a busy truck route, was eventually abandoned because of foreign protests). Seven nations – Russia, West Germany, Great Britain, Poland, Austria, Sweden and Bulgaria – sent teams, and there were also a number of individual competitors. The most famous of the individuals was the defending European Champion, HRH the Princess Anne, whose mount was the comparatively-inexperienced eight-year-old gelding Goodwill.

It seems to have surprised the Russian hosts that Princess Anne's participation drew the Western press like seagulls to a fishing trawler. According to one observer, 'They had expected them to be reporting on the horses, and found it strange that so many members of the press corps had come all the way to the USSR to photograph their own royal family.'

The British, favourites for the event and also the first foreign competitors to arrive in Kiev, came in for the brunt of the publicity and pressure. Most of the four team members and three individual riders were very young, and many were having their first experiences as ambassadors abroad. When in doubt they sheltered under the worldly wing of Princess Anne's detective, David Coleman, who was on excellent terms with the KGB. 'I can protect you against any crimes but two,' Mr Coleman explained to them one evening in their hotel. They waited, wondering what the Russians ranked with murder. 'Rape, and changing money on the black market,' Coleman went on. 'If you commit either of these I am powerless to help you.'

Other eye-openers came out of familiar happenings such as training problems. Lucinda, worried that work on the bone-hard ground might jar up her horse's feet, began to look around for cow dung, which, when mixed with clay, is cool and soothing.

'Four of us hired a car to collect cow dung to pack into Be Fair's feet,' she said. 'We had been told not to go off the main route, and the problem was that there were hardly any cows and what cows there were were so thin that there wasn't anything worth picking up. After two or three hours we spotted a fat cow on a peasant's patch, and stopped.

'I had forgotten to bring anything to take the cow dung home in, so searched around for some sort of container. Under the tree on the peasant's plot I found a German helmet, which must have been left there during the siege of Kiev. It had bullet holes in the skull.'

Aside from the hardness of the ground, which the Russians disc-harrowed under pressure the day before the cross-country, the most

KIEV 1973
Fence 2

Lucinda Prior-Palmer on Be Fair

The steep downhill approach to this notorious fence, giving inadequate room on the flat to gather momentum to clear the spread, caused 20 falls and 15 eliminations.

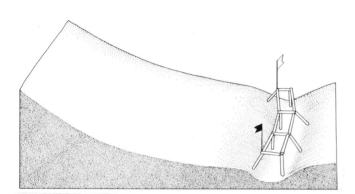

1. Driving hard into fence.
2. Note bundled power, and the distance the horse has to clear ahead.
3. Good forward momentum and balance.
4. Be Fair can't quite make it. Belly touches down on rail and repercussion bounces rider out of saddle.
5. Near hind leg was briefly caught behind rail. Horse maintains balance on front end alone while disentangling back leg. Rider's weight too far forward – could have been in trouble if horse had not made brilliant recovery.
6 and 7. Horse uses all of his body to get back into his stride, but not pleased with fence – note ears laid back.

Russian disasters at Fence 2.
This fence was a huge error
by the designer – rare in
eventing. Fortunately, no
horse was injured.

striking characteristic of Kiev was the severity of the second fence, at which half of the competitors fell, retired, or were eliminated. This was a classic example of a good course spoiled by a single over-ambitious obstacle. Huge parallel rails over a wide ditch, deep enough for a man to stand in, were approached from the most intimidating viewpoint – down a steep hill. It was a fence that could have been cleared easily, given sufficient speed; but the gradient of the downhill approach was so sharp that most horses came down slowly, more or less on their haunches. They had then only four or five strides on the level to gather the speed to carry them over. Many, not yet into rhythm so early in the course, thought twice about it, hesitated, and came into the wide spread without enough momentum. Most falls were caused by hitting the second parallel rail, but some hit the first and fell between the rails and into the ditch.

The best jump at fence 2 was by Russia's Alexander Evdokimov on the seven-year-old thoroughbred stallion Jeger. Dismissing the dangers of the precipitous approach, they came down with the speed of a late-night mail train and soared over the jump at a great gallop.

One of the most spectacular falls at the fence happened to Janet Hodgson and Larkspur. The horse dropped his back legs between the parallels, crashing down on the far side and catapulting his rider face-first into the landing. In ordinary circumstances they might have been expected to retire, since Janet was concussed and had three front teeth hanging loose; but, with Debbie West and Baccarat already out, retirement would have meant the British team's elimination. Janet remounted and jumped the remaining 28 fences, despite a further fall, losing much blood and gaining a rapidly-swelling face. This piece of heroism drew the applause it deserved, but also drew questions about whether it was fair to let girls compete over such stiff courses (the assumption seeming to be that, while men might knock their teeth out if they chose, women should not).

Only 22 of the 43 competitors completed the cross-country, and several teams were eliminated through failing to get three members round. West Germany won the team gold medal, Russia the silver, and Great Britain the bronze. Alexander Evdokimov, who had also performed the best dressage test, became the new individual European Champion. At the celebration party afterwards he was already back at work: he was a pop singer.

Burghley 1974 UK

World Championships, held every four years in the middle of what might otherwise be a doldrum period between Olympic Games, were introduced in 1966. The first was held at Burghley Park in Lincolnshire, following an invitation by the Fédération Equestre Internationale, the governing body of horse sports, to the British Equestrian Federation. Since then the Championships have been fought out in the country of the defending team.

The first World Championships were ruined by an outbreak of swamp fever, which eliminated all European entries from the competition. Only five countries sent teams, and of these only two, Ireland and Argentina, finished the trials. Captain Moratorio of Argentina, riding his own Chalan, became the first individual World Champion.

Four years later, in 1970 at Punchestown, Ireland failed to defend herself against teams from Argentina, France, West Germany, Great Britain and the USSR. Again, only two teams completed the course, Great Britain finishing well ahead of France. The individual champion was also British: Mary Gordon-Watson, riding her father's immense, bold-hearted Cornishman V, a horse who had been part of the Olympic gold-medal-winning team at Mexico two years before, and to whom the animal-crazy British public now gave the status accorded in most countries to a film star.

Cornishman did in fact eventually become a film star: after retiring from eventing he played the equine 'good guy' in the film of Dick Francis's novel, *Dead Cert*. The part called for him to jump over a saloon car – papier mâché, but painted to look real – and also over Becher's Brook, dread fence of the famous Grand National steeplechase; both of which, aged 16, he flew with the scorn of a horse accustomed to jumping really serious fences.

Having added the team and individual gold medals at the 1972 Olympics to this list of recent world supremacy, the British had every reason to feel complacent about their chances for the 1974 World Championships at Burghley. So that when the United States team turned up, equipped with all sorts of ridiculous American ideas – something called 'P & R' (pulse and respiration), which meant fiddling about with the horse's pulse and checking its breathing rate and taking its temperature before and after it worked . . . and something called 'Interval Training', which meant working the horse every fourth day and timing both the work and *rest* periods on a stop watch . . . and a *permanent team trainer*, of all things, who had worked with the team for the last *four years,* and other indications that the Americans were taking it *seriously* – well, the British were inclined to look on the whole thing as an amusing puppet show.

BURGHLEY 1974

Bruce Davidson and Irish Cap in action
during the 1974 World Championships.
LEFT: Show jumping on the final day.
BELOW: At the Trout Hatchery.
BOTTOM LEFT: Presentation of the trophy
by HRH the Duke of Edinburgh.
BOTTOM RIGHT: US team's lap of honour.

FAMILIAR FACES
AT BURGHLEY

Mary Gordon-Watson,
World Champion 1970.

LEFT: Lord Hugh Russell,
chairman of the British
selection committee, with
Major Peter Hodgson (left)
and Michael Naylor-
Leyland (seated).

OPPOSITE: Juliet Graham
and Sumatra (Canada) after
dressage. They were later to
become the highest-placed
Canadian individuals at the
Olympics, where they
finished in 11th place.
Background, Horst Karsten
and Sioux (West Germany).

Burghley, normally a national course second only to Badminton in size, went out of its way to produce a great World Championship cross-country with landings up banks, landings with drops, huge fences, lots of water, and a good number of combinations. Fence 5, the Double Coffin, was an exacting innovation. It had an approach palisade fence, 3′ 5″ high, built of tightly-packed upright logs so that the drop on the landing side was screened, two open ditches in the dip (5′ and 5′ 6″ wide), and a 3′ 11″ palisade jump out at the top of the final bank.

The most influential fence on the course was the famous Trout Hatchery water, part of the standard Burghley course, which came late in the cross-country when the horses were tiring. This year it offered a 3′3″ jump in, rising from the edge of the water as the last few feet of ground gave sharply away, thus making it difficult for the horse to remain on his hocks as he descended and prepared to take off, and a 3′9″ tree trunk on the way out of the holding water. The Trout Hatchery took its toll in eliminations, testing the slowing reactions of any horse and rider whose fitness was in any way questionable.

The ground was slightly sticky, summer-holding going, which is worse than winter-holding because the ground is heavy only on the surface, more binding than the slosh of winter mud. Many of the riders felt the labour but not Captain Mark Phillips, riding the Queen's Columbus, on whom he had won at Badminton earlier in the year. Captain Phillips, riding two different horses, had been a member of the winning British teams at Punchestown in 1970, at the European Championships in 1971 and at the 1972 Olympic Games. Now he put up the best cross-country score, and had it not been for a strained hock at one of the last fences which caused Columbus later to go lame and be withdrawn, might well have been the new World Champion.

So it was that the British, with a wealth of talent including the brilliant rider Richard Meade, a member of every British team since 1964 and Olympic Individual Gold Medallist at Munich, took on the French, Americans, the Irish, Germans, Austrians, Italians, the Russians, Poles and Swiss with confidence. Few but the well-informed paid more than passing notice to America's Bruce Davidson on Irish Cap, second at Ledyard Farm in 1973 to Susan Hatherly (GB), third at Badminton 74 to Phillips, and, on Plain Sailing, a member of the United States silver-medal-winning team at Munich.

Yet the precision of his performance, the discipline with which he and the other members of the US team obeyed the orders of their trainer, Jack Le Goff, whether these orders favoured them as individuals or otherwise, the whole mechanical, exact *perfection* of the American assault wiped the tolerant smile off British faces and left the home team trounced and vanquished. When the shock was over, the facts were unavoidable: the United States were the team World Champions. Bruce Davidson was individual World Champion.

'We suddenly realised that there was somebody else in the world

Burghley dressage: Bruce Davidson and Irish Cap.

who was on a par with the British, if not better,' Lucinda said later. She had spent time after the event digesting Davidson's generously-offered help with Interval Training methods. 'Suddenly three-day eventing was down to a T like a well-produced opera. The US just purred through, like a Mercedes in a field of Minis.'

Before Burghley 74 America had shown little interest in three-day eventing. Membership of the United States Combined Training Association was only 1500. After the World Championships, USCTA membership rose to over 10,000.

LUHMÜHLEN 1975
Water Jump

Sue Hatherly on Harley
Lucinda Prior-Palmer on Be Fair

1. Sue Hatherly and Harley (GB) over the upturned boat in the middle of the lake.

2. Lucinda Prior-Palmer and Be Fair landing over the boat.

3. Leaving the water: Sue and Harley.

4. Leaving the water: Lucinda and Be Fair.

5. The British silver-medal-winning team. Left to right: Princess Anne, Janet Hodgson, Lucinda Prior-Palmer, Sue Hatherly.

2

3

5

4

Luhmühlen 1975 FDR

The daggers of the 1975 European Championships were nicely cloaked, embellished with the thoughtful touches of a bride drooling over her first homestead. The irises in the water (artificial water, specially-planted irises) were perfectly in bloom; the thatching on the beehive fence was such a splendid work of art that all the folklore ever heard seemed suddenly substantiated. The gingerbread house come true.

Under the immaculate party dress the bones of the course were big, and clothed in startling combinations. One of the worst was the problem approaching and including the Normandy Bank, which had the extra difficulty of jumping from bright sunlight into and out of darkness. Three fences (23–25) were involved here: the first, a big brush into woodland, called for speed to clear it and courage to jump into the heavy gloom beyond; then, before the eyes had quite adjusted, a tree trunk followed at a right-angle, needing a sharp check in speed to make the turn. One stride beyond the tree trunk, moving on rising ground with much momentum lost by the check for the log, the sleepered face of the Normandy Bank needed precision riding to bring the horse up square on top for the jump out over the post and rails into bright sun and down the enormous drop. A number of horses stopped here, mainly through coming too fast over the brush approach fence and failing to make the turn over the tree trunk.

Fences 26, 27, 28 and 29, another combination, were a spectator's dream, though horses and riders who had got that far had little trouble with it. As one looked up the two great wood-faced banks each horse seemed microscopic at the top, cantering into first view over a post and rails approach and getting bigger as it dropped and dropped again towards the watcher, swinging right-handed at the bottom to push on over the stone-faced water trough, pump handle and all ... and, yes, a *real* stork's nest, or at least a believable one, sat in the branches of the left-hand tree beside the water trough.

Not all the horses got as far as that. Some went no farther than the water, number 6, where two alternative routes were offered: in on the left down a sleeper-faced bank preceded a stride back by posts and rails, up on to a wooden bridge at the half-way point of the lake and over low railings back into the water; or in on the right over rails and stream, a drop on to an 'island' and then over an upturned boat off the island down into the water. The mutual exit was up a bank and over a post and rails. Most riders, the German team excepted, favoured the right-hand route. Those who went left had trouble at the bridge, some because the horses would not try it and others through tripping over the exit railings.

The problems of varying light and shade were given full scope at Luhmühlen because of the brightness of the sunlight on cross-country day. In the patches of woodland, visibility by contrast was almost nil for a horse and rider cantering abruptly into shadow. Thus the formidable fence 22, giving an option of a double over a pair of palisades that hid some elegant rustic benches or a very big stretch over parallel palisades on the right-hand side (most riders chose the latter), provoked a lot of grief through semi-blindness.

Here, in the darkest stretch of woodland, Janet Hodgson, whose painful fall at Kiev two years before had done nothing to shake her nerve, went down for the second time on this course in a crashing somersault at the parallel palisades; got up reeling with concussion and typically went on to finish, though outside the time limit.

Two important by-products of an international championship seem curiously opposed, though both are vital to eventing as a world sport. By bringing together teams from many nations – at Luhmühlen France, Bulgaria, Great Britain, Ireland, Italy, Holland, Poland, Switzerland, Russia and West Germany – barriers are broken down despite the politics of each homeland and international friendships spring up from the sharing of the same dramatic challenge. Conversely, members of any one team who at home lead separate

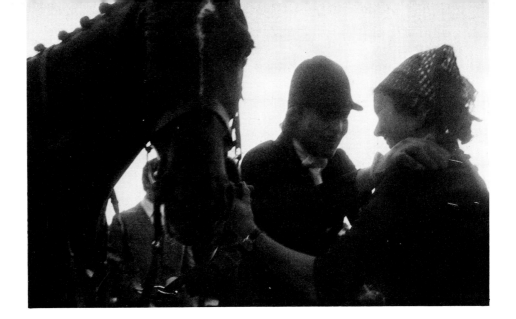

LEFT: Be Fair at the veterinary inspection, and, RIGHT, after the show jumping.

lives without especial thought for national unity are welded together in their country's name when four of them are far from home. It is for this reason that the team title is more zealously regarded than the individual prize, and because of it team trainers are able to command obedience that may be detrimental to individual achievement.

For example, horse 1 and horse 2 of a team have gone clear in good time, but horse 3 has been eliminated. The team is in a strong position: horse 4, the most brilliant on the team and yet to go, is good enough to win the individual gold medal. But horse X from another country has done so outstandingly well that horse 4 would have to pull out all the stops and take a lot of risks to beat it: if horse 4 takes these risks and falls, the chances of its team go with it. Therefore, despite horse 4's potential, the team trainer may order 'Steady, safe, and clear' and be obeyed.

Yet even though the trainer and each member of his team may do their utmost to safeguard their position as a unit, an element of chance is always present in eventing. Seldom has this been more apparent than in Luhmühlen, when, at the end of the cross-country, Britain was well ahead with a total of 198·20 penalty points against Russia's 233·00 and West Germany's 255·60.

Sunday, the show jumping day, was sunny; a lazy sort of day, a mere formality. Even if Russia went clear with all their members, Britain could knock three fences down and still retain the team gold medal. Because of Janet Hodgson's unfortunate elimination, Britain had only three team members left. The second to go, Sue Hatherly on Harley, seeing a long stride at the double, misjudged the distance, crashed through the first part, throwing Sue off ... the fall was counted also as a refusal at the second element. Altogether, 40 penalties; a disaster so unlikely that at the time the British hardly knew its weight.

The Russians went clear. So did Lucinda Prior-Palmer on Be Fair, the winners of the individual gold, and Princess Anne and Goodwill, who won the individual silver; but Britain, through a most unlikely accident, had lost its chance. The team gold medal went to Russia.

Ledyard 1975 USA

They came into Boston airport on an American-paid flight with ten days left to countdown, two German riders, two from Holland, six from England, their horses, relatives and grooms; all shell-shocked by American hospitality, spoiled silly by the generosity of Ledyard (in Europe an 'invitation' to compete often amounts only to free stabling for the horses).

Almost at once the party started, running from dawn to dusk with laughter in the blazing late-June weather. In the early mornings, before the sun was fairly up and flies came out to pester them, they took the horses out for work, riding at 5 or 6 o'clock when the air was fresh and cool. Each evening there were parties by a different host's pool. Three days before the dressage test, which no one could eventually remember, they had a clam-bake which got gloriously out of hand, where everyone, no matter how they ran and dodged and twisted, got thrown into the water (next day the pool was drained for rings and contact lenses). On Thursday, 26 June, heavy with happiness, tired and sunstruck, they pulled themselves together for the Briefing of Competitors.

Ledyard Farm, site of the biggest course in the United States, belongs to Mrs Frederick Ayer, mother of Neil Ayer, who is Director of Ledyard and also President of the United States Combined Training Association. According to Bruce Davidson, one of the few American riders to have had wide experience of foreign courses, Ledyard rates 'somewhere between Badminton and Burghley in severity'. It is a new course, inaugurated in 1973, and although not intended as a battleground for international championships it invites, in the fullest sense of the word, international competition.

The 1975 cross-country, designed by Richard Newton, was an excellent test of ingenuity and good galloping power. It was, overall, extremely well-built, offering a variety of clever problem fences at heights and spreads that were not so great that an up-and-coming horse might be discouraged.

The part that did the most undoing came halfway round, where, swinging along a woodland ride, the Coffin – thick slats to a height of 3'8", spaced far enough apart for a glimpse of the drop beyond, a five-foot ditch in the gully on to an upward rise to exit over another slatted fence (3'11") – eliminated several competitors. Long stretches of gallop, a test for an experienced rider, followed after, separating a conventional Table, a Normandy Bank, and a weird jump called the Picture Frame which asked for a three-foot jump through a wooden rectangle into a non-visible landing caused by a six-foot drop.

Most of the complicated jumps came early on, but 23, the Dragon's Moustache, called for assurance over the line of seven separate logs

The Ledyard winners, Bruce Davidson and Golden Griffin, were short-listed for the US Olympic team in 1976. Here they are at Bromont during the week before the competition started.

faced endways on towards the horse; and 26, the two- (or three-) part Stolen S, though low, needed a firm line to bounce through or cut across the corners.

OPPOSITE: Bruce Davidson and Royal Cor clearing a fence with plenty in hand.

The three days went as if stage-managed by a top suspense director, moving his cast around for maximum effect. When the curtain fell at the end of the first act (dressage), Mark Phillips and Laureate were out in front with a first-rate score of only 32·5 penalties, leading the German Herbert Blocker (Benson) and the home side's young Beth Perkins riding Furtive, a former Australian Olympic horse. On Saturday, cross-country day, Laureate got eliminated at the Coffin and Benson also dropped out of it by dubious virtue of refusals. The Saturday night results showed 18-year-old Beth Perkins seven points in front of Bruce Davidson on Golden Griffin, a horse he had only started riding a few days before the event. Third, Sue Hatherly and Harley, winners of Ledyard in its inaugural year, moved up to challenge.

Sunday, the show jumping, was performed in order from the least score to the highest. Some who had chances made a hash of it, tension becoming almost tangible as Davidson's other horse, Royal Cor, came up to fourth position. Harley, then Golden Griffin, jumped it clear. Last horse of all was Furtive, as good a mount cross-country as you could hope to meet but never much for show jumping; yet one by one the fences stood behind him ... until, three out, he dropped a shoulder and Beth Perkins hit the floor. It ended, as any movie-goer could have said it would, won by the home side's hero, Davidson.

Beth Perkins show jumping on Furtive.

Bruce Davidson and the American Revolution

Perspective distorts the importance of events in inverse proportion to the passage of time. Thus the rise of Genghis Khan (whose victories, incidentally, were largely due to his enormous travelling remuda of horses, used both as remounts and as food for his army) is less important in the twentieth century than the rise of the current Presidential candidate. Looking back over the history of three-day eventing during the first half of this century the first important happening, seen from the 1970s, is the crystallisation of dressage, steeplechase, endurance and show jumping into the French *Championnat du Cheval d'Armes* in March 1902. The last important happening of the half-century, chronologically undisputable no matter what history decides to make of it, was the birth of Bruce Davidson during the final hour and a half of 1949.

Davidson was born with an unwavering vocation to be a rider, a likely throwback to the Irish side of his Scottish–Irish family. Certainly this sense of the horse as the most important thing in life had skipped a generation or two, since neither his parents nor anyone else in his family showed the slightest interest in horses. As an adult, he looks back on this lack of family participation with an objectivity typical of his even approach to both success and disappointment: 'It had the advantage that I was never pushed as a rider, and the disadvantage that there was no one to share my enthusiasm.'

He began to ride at six years old, taking lessons in Massachusetts where his family owned a construction business. He was brought up on the eastern seaboard, a stroke of luck in many ways because of the variety of horse sports that were available to him as a child. 'I was raised where there was a lot of foxhunting, and went to boarding school in Maryland where we did one-day eventing,' he says, as if eventing were part of a normal school curriculum. His main scholastic achievement was as Captain of Riding, an honour he held for three years.

When the time came to go to college his continued belief that he must spend his adult life as a rider drew very natural opposition from

Bruce Davidson and Irish Cap during the dressage phase at Blue Ridge, Virginia, the last of the three United States Equestrian Team selection trials for the 1976 Olympics. Placed third in the first trial at Ship's Quarters, and easy winners at the interim Middletown trials despite show jumping faults, they were retired after winning the Blue Ridge dressage phase because team coach Jack Le Goff felt they had already proved themselves. It was an astonishing performance by Irish Cap, who had almost died from a lung complaint the previous year.

his family. National interest in eventing, the sport that had become of paramount interest to the teenage Davidson, was microscopic; therefore a career spent breeding and producing event horses when very few people were interested in buying them was, from his parents' point of view, not only stupid but, considering the construction boom and Bruce's prospects in the family business, spectacularly stupid. The compromise satisfied no one: Bruce applied to Iowa State University to become a student in veterinary medicine, was accepted, and during his so-called academic days spent much of his time eventing.

It is difficult to predict how long this family compromise could have continued had it not been for the effect on Davidson of the USCTA's belief that a permanent team trainer was essential for international success in eventing. Encouraged by team silver medals at both the Tokyo and Mexico Olympic Games, where they were trained respectively by Stefan von Vischy and Major John Lynch, the Americans had realised that the selection and development of promising horses and riders were an important part of a team trainer's

USET coach Jack Le Goff and Bruce Davidson. Without Le Goff's tenacity in choosing and welding together promising young riders the United States might never have re-emerged as a world power in eventing.

job. Although selectors of international teams for any country work from constant observation of a horse's public performances plus a great deal of inside information, those with no permanent trainer are faced with uncertainties which, to oversimplify the problems, run roughly along such lines as a) is the winner of a three-day event a brilliant horse moderately trained or a moderate horse brilliantly trained? or b) a horse has shown top national form by winning two good three-day events on reasonable ground: how will it act if, as at Mexico, there is a deluge during the cross-country? Concrete answers to questions such as these can come only from knowing the horse intimately, from observing the horse and its rider at close quarters over several months, and the American argument for a permanent team trainer has as much foundation in periods of residence of the prospects under the trainer's eye as it has to do with the ultimate welding together of four individuals into a team. The trainer elected to this full-time post while Davidson was still at Iowa State was a Frenchman, Jack Le Goff.

Le Goff, a former French army instructor, had as blue-blooded a background as could be wished for in any trainer. Born in 1932, the son of a cavalry officer, he won the *Championnat National du Cheval de Selle* (formerly the *Championnat du Cheval d'Armes*) in 1956, and the *Championnat de France de Concours Complet* (formerly the *Championnat National du Cheval de Selle*) in 1963. Adjutant-Chef Le Goff's 1963 mount, Mon Clos, won the *Championnat* again in 1965, this time ridden by Adjutant Jean-Jacques Guyon, and the Le Goff-trained horse Pitou, also ridden by Guyon, won the individual gold medal at Mexico in 1968. Le Goff had further coached the French Olympic team to Mexico, where they finished fourth, had been a successful jockey both on the flat and over the sticks, had spent ten years as chief instructor at Saumur, and since 1965 had coached both the French senior and junior teams. In February 1970 he arrived in America as the newly-appointed team trainer to the United States. In the spring of that year, spotting what he felt was a remarkable talent, he invited 20-year-old Bruce Davidson to stay with him for several months for observation and training.

Finally convinced of Bruce's whole-hearted commitment to eventing, his family agreed that he might study under Le Goff, though with the provision that if he failed to make it he would have to dismiss eventing as the foremost focus of his life (since then they have become enthusiastic supporters of his choice of career). At the United States Equestrian Team training centre in Gladstone, New Jersey, Bruce met Carol Hannum, daughter of Judge Hannum of Pennsylvania and of his foxhunting wife, the Master of Mr Stewart's Cheshire Foxhounds. Carol, who had been short-listed for the Olympic team in 1968 and who was later (1972) to ride her horse Paddy to be leading points winner in the US, became Bruce's girlfriend and, in January 1974, his wife.

Dropping out of Iowa State made about as much ripple in Davidson's consciousness as a pebble thrown into a rough sea.

His whole concentration was focussed upon eventing, and in particular upon Le Goff and the novel method of training horses that the Frenchman was propounding – Interval Training.

Interval Training has been practised successfully by human athletes for many years. It is based on a constant but gradual increase in the power of the subject's heart, lungs and muscles and on a thorough knowledge and continual check on the 'normal' development of each subject. There is no reason why it should not be applied to any mammal. Davidson summarises it as follows:

'The principle of Interval Training is to put a certain amount of stress and strain on the heart and lungs, to rest the horse not quite to normal, and then to work it again so that its power is built up rather than remaining constant or decreasing. It seems to work on a four-day cycle, maybe because the result of work does not necessarily show in the legs until the fourth day; so that if on the third day after working you gallop a horse and on the fourth you find him unsound the damage may have been caused by the first day's work and may only have been compounded by work done on the third day.'

For Interval Training to be practised most efficiently the horse's normal pulse and respiration rates must first be established (P & R, a widespread technique in the training of modern racehorses that is sometimes looked on by conservative horsemen as so much new-fangled mumbo-jumbo, merely means taking a horse's pulse and counting its respiration rate before and after it gallops). In building up a complete picture of the horse's basic physical condition it is obviously also useful to establish its normal temperature, which varies slightly from animal to animal just as it does in humans.

At rest the horse will have a pulse rate somewhere between 32 and 40 beats a minute. Cantering tends to increase the flow of circulation of the blood by a factor roughly one-and-a-half times the normal rate, or slightly more; a short gallop may push the pulse up to 100, using up oxygen in the bloodstream at two-and-a-half times the normal speed. The amount of work that a horse can stand depends upon the capacity of its heart and lungs to supply oxygen into the blood and to remove the lactic and carbonic acids formed by the oxidization of glucose as heat energy in the muscles. Thus, knowledge of how hard the horse's heart and lungs have to work to sustain, say, a two-minute gallop gives an exact picture of the development of those organs. If all this sounds complicated, so it is – many successful practitioners of Interval Training do not work on such demanding measurements, but rely solely on their intuitive knowledge of their horse.

When a horse is overstrained it is because the heart and lungs cannot maintain a sufficient supply of oxygen to the muscles and cannot carry away the accumulating acids fast enough, causing the muscles to lose their elasticity. The first symptom of this accumulated acid, as any unfit person who has tried to run a mile will know, is that the legs ache. Taken to excess, the supply of blood to the legs gets less and less, and in the moment of absolute exhaustion cuts off completely. Autopsies performed on horses destroyed at the time of breaking down have shown the blood vessels white – bloodless – on the damaged leg.

Any reasonable form of physical training will increase the performance of the heart and lungs and develop the muscles, but a haphazard approach to fitness is likely to work against itself at times by undoing the power it has built up either through too much stress or through too much relaxation. For example, walking for two hours a day for seven days will mean that at the end of the week the horse/human/dog is fitter than at the start. Running for ten miles on the eighth day will probably mean that the subject can hardly move on the ninth; conversely, leave off the exercise for a week, then walk for two hours – the walker will have lost condition and will not find it as easy as he found it seven days before. It takes three to four days for a horse's body – his ligaments, tendons and muscles – to return to normal after strain has been endured. Interval Training works on a sustained build-up of the physique, ensuring that the subject is worked at the precise point at which he has had not quite sufficient rest to be back at his starting point and that the amount of work is increased gradually as the capacity of the body develops. In horses, it at once helps to prevent the animal from breaking down through not exposing him to too much stress and ensures, by measuring each effort, that lazy animals work. There is, of course, more to it than that.* For an example of Interval Training in practice see page 72.

Under the tutorship of Jack Le Goff, Davidson soaked up Interval Training like a hungry sponge. Soon it became second nature. When the lack of facilities in America ('Americans don't get to ride enough big courses. Britain has Badminton and Burghley to produce young horses and to keep riders up to scratch,' he says enviously) forced the United States team to train in England for the 1972 Olympics, he was astonished at the casual training methods of the opposition. 'How can you expect to get a horse fit by galloping through woods full of rabbit holes?' he asked the British riders. 'What horse is going to stand up to a three-day event when it's effectively *done* a three-day event twice a week in its training for the last four weeks before competing?' England won the Munich team gold medal, the United States the silver, and Davidson's and Le Goff's radical training methods were by and large dismissed in Europe as being without foundation. One of the few who had begun to listen was Lucinda Prior-Palmer, who, in 1970, had trained by cantering for 40 minutes with two one-mile gallops in each session. In 1972 Lucinda's canters were cut to 30 minutes at a stretch, and by 1973, when she won Badminton for the first time, to 25.

Davidson's victory in the 1971 Eastern Canadian Championship on the USET's Plain Sailing and his subsequent part, on the same horse, in winning the team silver at Munich had begun to bring him an international reputation. His third at Badminton in 1974 on Irish Cap, after a session spent with his wife at Wylye, Wiltshire, on

Effective Horsemanship, G. N. Jackson, (David Rendel, London, 1967).

Mike Plumb, silver medallist at Burghley World Championships on Good Mixture and 1976 Olympic silver medallist on Better and Better, competing on Vanier at Blue Ridge in 1974.

1974 National Junior Champion, Cindy Irwin, on Bonanza's Little Dandy at Hillview one-day event, 1975.

Torrance Watkins and Red's Door at the Palisade, last fence on the Blue Ridge Olympic selection course, 1976.

Acclimatising at Bromont during the week before the 1976 Olympic Games, Bruce Davidson on Golden Griffin and Mike Plumb on Better and Better.

the excellent training grounds owned by Lord and Lady Hugh Russell, underscored his promise. But it was the total defeat of England on its home ground, Burghley, in the 1974 World Championships by the United States, who won the team gold medal and both the individual gold (Davidson) and the individual silver (Michael Plumb), that forced the Europeans to recognize the success of the Interval Training method. This recognition was underscored by the relatively minor interest in eventing in America (USCTA membership in 1974 about 1500, UK Combined Training membership roughly 2600), showing that with fewer riders to choose from and fewer home facilities to bring them on Jack Le Goff could nonetheless produce a winning team.

The aftermath of the 1974 World Championships was a tremendous growth of interest in eventing in North America. Davidson's subsequent win at Ledyard and his silver medal at the 1975 Pan American Games, American equivalent of the European Championships, fell into perspective as part of the continuing development of one of the outstanding event riders of the century, and his and Carol's venture into the business of breeding and producing event horses on their working farm in Pennsylvania no longer seemed unpracticable. On the international scene, these proofs of dedication, planning and overall improvement in the techniques of training strengthened the qualities of competition in every country seriously interested in eventing.

Starting from Scratch

The first seriously uncomfortable moment for the newcomer to eventing comes on signing the cheque for the horse. Usually a considerable sum is being paid for an animal whose past is uncertain and whose ability to perform in events has never been put to the test. That the seller may be asking a high price for it is no indication of its worth. Unlike a car a horse has no fixed book value, and despite the most thorough of veterinary examinations essential qualities such as its courage cannot be assessed by looking under the bonnet.

Because so many variables exist there can be no absolute definition of a good event horse in the making. A youngster sired by a proven getter of event horses or out of an event-winning mare has at least the possibility of an inherited inclination towards eventing (this possibility will be reflected in its price), but until the new owner has worked with it himself for a year or two he will never be quite sure whether or not he has bought the right horse. The young horse potentially suitable for eventing is usually a well-grown animal standing 16–16·2 hands high, having good bone and conformation, and being very nearly but not quite thoroughbred. Pure thoroughbreds are apt to be highly-strung and may be too excitable, when fit, to settle well enough to do a good dressage test. One eighth, or even a quarter, of hunter blood or similar often adds an invaluable touch of calmness and toughness. It also means that the horse is a less expensive gamble, since seven-eighths-bred horses are not registered.

The best time to buy the horse, unless the purchaser has adequate home facilities to bring on a very young animal cheaply, is when it is four years old. By then it will have matured sufficiently for elementary work to be started on it, while you will not have the extra expense of keeping it for another slow-maturing year. You will also be buying the horse before anyone else has begun to do serious work with it. A horse that is more than four years old could be suspect if it is put up for sale, as it is possible that the seller or someone else has tried the horse out and found it wanting in some respect, perhaps discovering that it will not jump water or that it is lacking in courage. Even if an

OPPOSITE: Lucinda and Be Fair at home.

older animal is being sold for a genuine reason – its owner, for instance, might be unable to continue riding – there is still no way of knowing what harm may have been done to it by its previous rider – how hard the horse may have been forced on, or what bad habits may have been induced or confirmed in it.

The essentials of a young event prospect can be colloquially defined as class and guts. Class, the indefinable quality of style that will take the eye of the dressage judge, is mandatory in the modern event horse. In the not-far-distant past it was possible to do a bad dressage test, complete the cross-country phase at top speed and win an event quite easily, but today the best scorer in the dressage is usually also among the best cross-country. With the all-round rise in standards, it is often at once the best schooled horse, the best ridden, the best fed and the best kept.

Provided the young horse has class, the way it moves is less important. An attractive mover is an apparent asset, but more vital than its natural grace is the power of its movement – its power to jump, gallop and cover ground. It is not necessary for the horse naturally to throw its toes out prettily, as it can be taught, by schooling, to produce the long, easy stride that dressage judges like. In some ways the not-so-elegant mover is a better buy, because those that are naturally extravagant movers can be hard to train; they throw their toes out automatically without doing any work, and so are difficult to get in hard condition, possibly proving, when put to the test, that they are neither as fit nor as settled as the rider had been led to assume. Conversely, a horse that is not a natural mover has to be well worked in before it will use its shoulders properly, bring out its feet and extend its paces, and so it is less likely to blow up during the dressage test.

Natural balance, however, is a valuable bonus in a novice horse. Ideally, the point of balance should be in the centre of the horse – if the natural point is forward of centre it will need a long time and an experienced rider to bring the balance back to a position from which the horse can perform really well.

Guts in a horse are extremely difficult to gauge. Some horses can be cowards despite the most immaculate upbringing, while others may have been ridden by someone nervous enough to encourage the horse to stop at a fence, or by a rider so frightened that he has beaten the horse into its fences, in which case the horse will have learned to rush his fences and hurl himself over without thinking. A prospective purchaser should always try the horse over a fence or two when he first inspects it. If the horse goes badly, his subsequent decision on whether or not he may be able to correct whatever fault it has shown may be extremely uncomfortable.

The safest solution for a rider who is a comparative novice and who is offered an uncertain jumper is not to buy it. No four-year-old, because of its age, is going to know much about jumping, and most may make mistakes in judging even very simple fences, but a horse that stops naturally or has learned to stop is usually very difficult to cure. Often, despite the most searching psychology, the rider will never be able to find out why a horse stops; though, particularly in the case of refusals at idiosyncratic fences such as small ditches, a young horse may simply be expressing unfamiliarity or wilfulness, displaying a natural instinct to avoid objects that might offer cover for a predator or maybe an assertion of its own personality over its rider's wishes which could in the long run develop into a desirable cross-country boldness.

A horse that 'scotches' or 'props' into its fences, shortening its stride as it approaches, obviously wondering about the jump but nonetheless getting over somehow, is a readier proposition. Such a horse can usually have its faults corrected quite easily by an experienced rider, can be taught to have confidence in its jumping ability, to lengthen its stride, and to be obedient to the wishes of its rider. Since most novice event riders are young people who cannot be expected to have had sufficient experience to be able to straighten out a horse which is a sticky jumper, the wisest course of action with a potentially good but ignorant horse is to hand it over at once to a veteran who is used to bringing on novices.

Just as novice horses may be harmed by novice riders, so may

Be Fair at three years old. Good points: broad forehead, sloping shoulder, depth of girth, the long distance from point of hip to hock, and the straight line from point of buttock to hock to fetlock, indicating a strong hind leg.
Bad points: long cannon bones (tendons could be overstrained) and distrustful look in eye.

A typical novice horse, just broken. Be Brave, four years old, jumping for the first time over something more serious than cavaletti.

novice riders be harmed by novice horses. Many of the best horse-and-rider combinations in eventing have started out with the arrival of a big, raw birthday present for a teenager who has neither the experience nor the physical strength to manage it. In such situations fright is not only natural but sensible. The solution, again, is to send the horse to someone strong enough to teach it manners, and the sooner this is done the less chance there is that the horse may have time to acquire or enforce bad habits.

Either way – with the horse kept at home or sent elsewhere – the first winter of the four/five-year-old's life is usually best spent in the hunting field, not hunting strenuously. Its legs will not harden up thoroughly until it is six or seven years old, and the longer it is left to mature the more soundness a horse will have left at the end of its life. The object of hunting it – which may come in for disapproval from other members of the field who look on hunting as the ultimate purpose of a horse and not as a training ground for potential event horses – is to get the horse going freely across country, loving the idea of jumping whatever comes in its way, developing a catlike cleverness over its fences and improving its general knowledge and courage. A young horse ridden upsides a bold, reliable jumper at the head of the field, jumping its fences either behind a guaranteed leader or at least not behind a horse that may set a bad example by stopping, will probably learn more in one season in the hunting field than it would in two or three years of jumping in cold blood by itself.

It is advisable very early on to get the young horse into the habit of doing its dressage at the start of each exercise period, going straight from the stable into the school before it has got its back down rather than by taking the easy way out and settling it with road work before asking it for such precise obedience. Later on, when it reaches the eventing stage, the value of habitual dressage, no matter how fresh the horse is feeling, will make it easier to settle the horse for the dressage test when, hard fit and full of itself for the cross-country, it comes straight from the horsebox or stable into a new and exciting environment. Depending on the prowess of the individual animal, routine dressage practice may last from 15 minutes to two hours – until the horse is going presentably, has gone through its movements or understood whatever new movement is required of it. School work should not be carried on to the point at which the horse becomes bored, but should be stopped when the horse has carried out its work harmoniously (or at least has tried to do so), and can be praised for its efforts.

At this stage, as in all subsequent stages, the young event rider should be handling his horse himself, getting to know the individual peculiarities of the animal while at the same time increasing his general knowledge of all aspects of horsemastership. Regular instruction from one or more trainers is essential. Even riders who have reached advanced stages of dressage will regress without a ground jockey to criticise them, as it is never possible to be sure how

Be Brave, with Lucinda, spooking over a fence. Note the concentrated interest of a very green horse questioning an obstacle.

69

one may look through other people's eyes, and faults in a rider's seat occur so gradually that he is not aware of their development. If a rider must work by himself for much of the time and if he is lucky enough to have an indoor school or barn in which to work, a mirror fitted on the wall will help him to perfect his own position.

No one, no matter how experienced, would claim to know everything about a horse or about riding. Working with a number of trainers, whether or not they are specialists in different branches of horsemanship, will give a rider wider opportunities to benefit from the experience of other people than he would have if he limited himself to only one advisor. There is also the additional benefit that a trainer may take more notice of his pupils if he has only a limited number of lessons in which to sort them out.

In the spring of its five-year-old year, if the horse has matured well and is going freely across country, hunter trials and riding club events in the early part of the season will lay a solid foundation for one or two novice one-day events towards the end of the spring. The object of these events lies not in winning but in teaching the horse his job, and great care should be taken to ensure that he is not forced ahead of his ability nor allowed to become over-excited by his strange surroundings. He should be rewarded when he does well, and even when he finishes far down the card there are usually one or two moments in the day when he has done his best. Praise for his overall effort, no matter what the final score, gives him comfort and induces a pleasant association with his job.

During the summer the horse should be turned away for two or three months at grass so that he can be thoroughly rested. Bring him up ten weeks before his first novice event in the autumn, and walk him steadily for one to two hours a day for two weeks to get the grass fat off him, to get his system used to the new hard food, and his body ready for the start of the new training season. Four or five novice events in the autumn should be quite enough to ask at this stage. After that he should be turned away again until midwinter, rested in the field unless he has been sticky over the autumn's cross-country fences. Hunting for a second season will underscore the experiences picked up during the winter of his four-year-old year, but if he is going well in novice events he will now be too valuable to risk in the hunting field.

By this time it is usually, though not necessarily, possible to know how the horse is shaping as a three-day event prospect, though there are horses who will perform with perfect satisfaction at this stage but who will later, and for no obvious reason, object to any course higher than novice standard. Bad signs to look for are such as if the horse stops in hot blood, becomes 'windy', or is unsound. It is a waste of investment, both of time and money, to ditch a horse as soon as things begin to go wrong, since the fault is more likely to lie with the jockey than with the horse – lack of fundamental ground work, the wrong food, inadequate physical preparation, disorganised routine (horses thrive on regular hours and are disturbed by irregular feed and exercise times), and so on. Only if the rider has repeated reason to suspect that his horse is either gutless or unsound should the animal be abandoned without further waste of time.

During its second season, if all is going well, the horse should again be started off in novice events and, if it performs satisfactorily, can be upgraded to intermediate. By the end of the spring it may possibly be ready for a three-day event at intermediate standard, though this is asking a lot of a six-year-old. After its summer holiday at grass it can be trained up for more intermediate events, one-day or three depending on its rider's judgment; and if it shows exceptional promise it might compete in an open event, though generally even the most talented horses will not yet be ready for such a demanding performance. An acceptable all-round test at intermediate level during the autumn is as much as can be hoped for from a six-year-old, and if the horse produces this its rider has every reason for feeling satisfied.

In the third year of the horse's training, after its winter holiday, it should be brought up nine or ten weeks before its first one-day event or 12 to 14 weeks before its first three-day event. If it has done exceptionally well in its last season it may conceivably be ready for a top-class national event at open, intermediate or advanced standard; but it is safer not to force the horse at this stage of training, rather to reinforce its progress by not asking too much of it while it is still learning. Only the rider, knowing the difficulties of national courses and of courses in other countries, can tell which three-day event will now best suit his horse.

At eight years old the horse should be arriving at the point of readiness for a top-class three-day event, but you should bear in mind that it is still learning and that event horses do not usually reach their peak until they are 11 or 12 years old. At six years old so much is happening to the horse, so much physical and mental experience is yet to come, that serious damage can be done if heavy strain is asked of it. Its bones and body, as well as its brain, need time to mature if it is to make the grade in top-class competition.

Interval Training for a Three-Day Event

A training programme for a specific three-day event at advanced or international standard calls for about 14 weeks of work from the field to the course to achieve the level of hard fitness that will be needed during the final stages of the speed and endurance test. A precise plan of action should be worked out beforehand, listing what work will be done and when, and also keeping an exact record of what has already been done with the horse in its day-by-day routine.

A wall chart, file chart, or any piece of paper big enough to cover the whole 14 weeks with sufficient space for each day's comments will not only help as a reminder of what has been done with the horse but will pinpoint minor setbacks in the training programme, variations in temperature, when the horse was last shod, and so on. It will also provide useful hindsight on such things as how the horse performed in deep going, how it reacted to a new kind of horse nuts or a different bridle, and may show up weaknesses in its overall training programme, such as a reluctance to jump drop fences due to insufficient practice. When the horse is being trained for a big event it is fairly easy to overlook the fact that its first three-quarter peak of fitness must be reached about a month before the main objective, when its plan will probably include one or two warm-up or team selection one-day events. Putting these secondary events in large letters on the horse's chart should make such oversights impossible.

In planning a programme for an event the first requisite is for the rider to ensure that he has made the proper applications to his country's governing body of eventing, that his subscriptions are paid up so that he and his horse are eligible for entry, and that entries have been posted off for the events at which he means to compete. Reading the fine print of the rules for each event can save much disappointment later on, when a rider can find that after all the work he has put into training his horse may not conform to the conditions of entry.

While the horse's training is going on, equal importance must be attached to getting the rider fit. Physical exercises such as running, skipping, cycling, galloping on racehorses (if available) to clear the rider's wind and strengthen his lungs, squash or tennis, habits such as running upstairs on the toes instead of on the ball of the foot, and of course abundant riding all help to prepare the body for the demands that will be made on it during a three-day event. A healthy diet, and in many cases a weight-reducing one, will both ensure that the horse does not have to carry weight in excess of the standard 165lbs and that the rider is not handicapped by loose weight on his body.

The horse's diet is equally important. Coming up from grass he should at first be fed on low-protein nuts or on only small amounts of oats until his body has hardened to the point where he can cope with the release of energy provided by high protein feed. Too much protein in the early stages, or on rest days when the horse has no opportunity to work off the food he is given, may result in azoturia, familiarly called 'Monday morning sickness', which appears as a startling, sudden lameness or partial paralysis during exercise.

Feed should start at the equivalent of six to 10lbs of oats a day when the horse begins to work, increasing to around 16lbs when the horse is eventing fit. Precise quantities of each ingredient vary according to the taste of the horse, but most horses will become bored when fed an unmixed diet. Most horses appreciate appetisers such as chopped or grated carrot or apple mixed into their feed, and all will benefit from added vitamin supplements. A bran mash twice a week, containing boiled linseed, whole oats and barley, cleans out the intestines and should be fed on the evening before a rest day, after the horse has worked. Difficult eaters, assuming the cause is not ascribable to some physical reason such as overlong teeth, call for experiment to find out what it is in the feed that they dislike. If they are persistently fussy about their food their attitude may be changed by making them miss a feed every now and then, so that they go hungry. Limiting the amount of hay fed will make a horse hungrier in the morning, more ready to clean up its breakfast feed, and this limitation (or in some cases total abstinence) from hay may help against the dry cough often produced when dust in the hay gets into the windpipe and causes irritation. Hay that has been damped down or soaked in a bin of water so that the dust cannot rise is often of great help to a cougher. Most authorities would agree that a certain amount of hay is needed to provide bulk food, but this has proved to be not necessarily always the case.

Since a horse's stomach is relatively small in relation to the animal's size, food should be given little and often. Four feeds a day, at, say, 7am, noon, 4pm and 7pm, are advisable, and it is important that the times of feeding should remain constant. Bran added to two of the four feeds makes a change, but its food value is low and its price is often uneconomic. Fresh water should be abundantly available – many horses will drink two bucketsful overnight.

The precise training programme of the horse varies according to the knowledge, experience and theories of its trainer, according to available time and available facilities and also to individual quirks of the horse (or trainer). The programme given here is the one that was

It is not only the horse that has to train. Lucinda Prior-Palmer bicycles round Badminton.

used to train Lucinda Prior-Palmer's chestnut gelding Be Fair for the European Championships at Luhmühlen in September 1975, at which he won the individual gold medal. It is an example of Interval Training in practice, is based on what Lucinda learned from Bruce Davidson, and no suggestion is intended that it will automatically suit every horse as well as it obviously suited Be Fair. 'No one,' Lucinda says, 'ought to write down training methods as a dictation of what to do, but simply as a basis from which to discuss how best to train a horse. There are so many different ways to achieve the same object – that of a fit horse ready to win. The more one looks and listens, the more one learns.'

Be Fair came up from grass 14 weeks before Luhmühlen. For the first two weeks he was walked steadily on the roads to get the grass fat off him and to harden up his legs. Exercise began with only one hour a day, and by the end of the first week had steadied out at two hours. The horse was ridden for six days a week and had one day off for rest. After exercise, if the weather was fine, he was turned out in the paddock for half an hour or more to relax.

The next two-and-a-half weeks were devoted to quiet rides on the hills, walking on the roads, and occasionally a little cantering. Be Fair was trotted on grass but never on the road, as Lucinda felt it might impose an unnecessary jar. Three or four times a week she would do some light schooling to supple the horse and improve his dressage. In the middle of the fifth week Be Fair began his Interval Training programme, starting his first work day with a steady working canter at 15 mph for three minutes, with a two-minute break and then a final three-minute canter. Duration of canters and break were timed on a stop-watch. 'At the start,' Lucinda says, 'the horse must be taught to relax during each break. If necessary get off him and let him pick grass.'

The length of the break is as important as the length of each canter, since the principle of Interval Training is that the second effort comes just before full recovery after the first; so that the *extra* effort therefore required by the second canter expands the lungs and uses the whole body that much more, thus progressively increasing the horse's capacity.

Over the next seven weeks Be Fair's canters were worked up at an average of one every four days until he was eventually covering seven or eight miles at a slow but working canter (15 mph equals four minutes to the mile). As the number of minutes worked increased, Lucinda split the canters into three with a three-minute break between each. 'As the horse becomes fit he should have stopped blowing by the end of the first break, and by the end of the second break he should be doing no more than moving under the ribs.'

Lucinda's principle was that fast work should be done only in the three to four weeks preceding the three-day event, though in this example of Be Fair's training for Luhmühlen a two-day event at Osberton three weeks before the Championships meant that he started to gallop earlier. Sixteen days before Osberton – that is, four

OPPOSITE: Much of the preparatory work for an event happens in the tack room and at the desk.

work days ahead of the event – he went into work. Fast work was limited to just enough to make the horse blow, and was started at around three furlongs and increased in the last two gallops to three-quarters of a mile. On the bases of both her own teenage experiences and of observation of others, Lucinda feels that many people over-gallop their horses. She prefers to make her horse blow by trotting or cantering up hills rather than by pounding along at a three-quarter-speed gallop. 'Everyone has different ideas and ideals. Mine are continually altering, because they are made up of a mixture of other people's ideas and experiences and reasonings.'

Be Fair's Interval Training proceeded on the classic four-day work-plan. The day after working (Day 1, if one assumes starting from the lowest point and working up to Day 4 as the canter day) was rest day. On Day 1 Be Fair was either ridden at a walk or was turned out. On Days 2 and 3 he was exercised for 60 to 90 minutes, usually practising dressage and doing steady road work, with sometimes some show jumping or an occasional cross-country fence. Most days, since it was a consistently fine summer, he was turned out for half an hour or so after exercise.

His work programme, following his initial working canter during his fifth week up from grass of three minutes interspersed by a two-minute break, and followed by another three minutes of work, was developed every fourth day in this progression:

Four minutes canter, three minutes break, four-and-a-half minutes canter (Be Fair, who had long before learned to relax, was walked during each break rather than dismounted);

Three minutes canter, three minutes break, four minutes canter, three minutes break, four minutes canter (after this, all breaks were of three minutes duration);

Four minutes canter, (three minutes break), five minutes canter, (three), five minutes canter;

Five minutes, (three), five-and-a-half minutes, (three), six minutes;

Six, (three), six, (three), six-and-a-half;

Seven, (three), eight, (three), seven-minute canter plus half-mile gallop;

Eight, (three), nine, (three), eight plus five-furlong gallop;

Ten, (three), ten, (three), nine plus six-furlong gallop;

Ten, (three), ten, (three), four plus six-furlong gallop – the slight decrease in cantering time being because this last day of work came four days before the Osberton two-day event, which Be Fair won.

After Osberton he had an easy week, spent only walking until he was taken up to Ascot for a week of training with other team members for the European Championships under the guidance of the British chef d'équipe Colonel Bill Lithgow. It was the first time that Interval Training had been seen in practice in England, and Lucinda's novel methods came in for a lot of laughter. Colonel Lithgow, who wanted the team to gallop one-and-a-half miles round Ascot racecourse, suffered resistance from most of his trainees and an absolute refusal from Lucinda. 'All right, Lucinda,' he conceded good-humouredly, 'if you win the individual gold next week we'll have to think again! You can go at the end of the session, when everyone else has worked, and do your tribal rites.'

Be Fair's one work day at Ascot consisted of nine, (three), nine, (three), four plus a half-mile gallop. Just before shipping out to Germany six days before the competition he was given a sharp five-furlong gallop.

In Germany, seemingly fitter than he had ever been before, he was taken along gently, schooled a little, walked a lot on long, quiet interesting rides so that he became adapted to his new surroundings, alert and interested, happy and well and beginning to feel the need to run. Four days before the cross-country, apart from a blow out later after the dressage test, he did his only piece of work: one-and-a-half furlongs uphill at a gallop. At the end of the Championships Lucinda reported that he had never been fitter or felt keener to jump.

Many riders feel that regular cantering and galloping in the few days leading up to a three-day event is beneficial. Lucinda disagrees: 'In the last week I like to *diminuendo* my horse. I would rather have the horse fit by the week-end preceding the three-day event and then, apart from a good sharp two-furlong pipe-opener after the dressage test before cross-country day, only do slow but interesting work, if necessary for long periods if the horse has an excitable temperament. The horse will not lose fitness without fast work during those few days, though maybe exceptions would have to be made with horses that were not thoroughbred or that were very thick-winded.

'A great deal of the *au point* fitness lies in the mental side of it. A horse that has not had to work very hard during the last few days will go all the better for its freshness on cross-country day. The pipe-opener after the dressage test should be quite enough to gee it up for the cross-country.'

IN ACTION

At Any Event

ONE-DAY
EVENTS

From the spectator's angle it looks neat and unfrenetic. At various stages during the event the rider appears in one of two or three elegant costumes, the horse, seemingly assured, immaculate, calm and brave, performs three very different tests with minor adjustments to its clothing. Presumably, if it is thought about at all, they came from somewhere and, like the spectator, after the event will travel home.

What happens behind the composed front during the one or two days of a one-day event is relentless hard work. During the four or five days of a three-day event it is hard work interspersed with distracting periods of free time which can give a worrier plenty of room for indulging his disability.

Assuming a one-day event that is not so heavily entered that the dressage has to take place the day before, the order of the day for most competitors allows no time for sitting around. If at all possible, getting another person to drive the horsebox to the event helps to conserve energy that the rider will have need of later on. On first arrival it is prudent for someone to go to the Secretary's tent and pick up a programme and a number cloth. As soon as possible the horse, who will very likely be wondering where he is, should be unboxed and ridden around on a loose rein to let him look about and accept his new surroundings. Ride him as near as is allowed to the dressage arena to show him the area where he will shortly be performing. When he has settled he can be worked or lunged until he is fluid, obedient and relaxed. He may be given a short pipe-opener later, after his dressage test.

After the horse has been returned to the horsebox the rider must walk the show jumping and cross-country courses if he has not contrived to do this the day before. In most one-day events show jumping comes before cross-country, which is easier on both horse and rider because the discipline of the tight vertical leaps comes after the horse has been thoroughly ridden in for dressage and not after he has been asked to extend for the longer, flatter, faster jumps he will have to perform cross-country. Walking the show jumping course requires thought about the best place to turn into a fence, which is

OPPOSITE: Handicaps of a very light rider. Debbie West weighs out. Note massive weight cloth, packed with lead in pockets, under saddle.

BADMINTON 1976
Quarry, Steps and Ramp

Chris Collins on Smokey VI

2

4

5

A superb jump by a man who has twice been Champion Amateur Steeplechase Jockey. By keeping close contact, he maintains perfect balance of his horse while giving it complete freedom.

A bank up needing judgment because there is not room on top to reposition the horse to meet the 3′ palisade fence. Speed for the two upward leaps needs careful control because the landing is on a sharply-sloped downhill ramp.

1. Controlled leap on to the bank.

2. Rider takes a steadying pull with his hands while continuing the forward pressure with his legs, resulting in…

3. a low, balanced descent over the palisade. Note how far Chris has slipped his reins.

4. Weight on stirrup irons, leaning back to keep centre of gravity on the drop. Strong grip through knee into stirrups.

5. The left hand is freed to shorten the reins.

6

6. Only one-ninth of a second later the left hand has shot forward to pick up the reins and get into gear for the turn to the Quarry Wall.

BADMINTON 1976
Quarry, Steps and Ramp

Aly Pattinson on Olivia

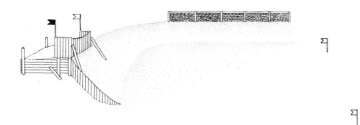

2

4

Same fence as the page before, but a different story. Olivia is a very impetuous little mare, and a ducking in the Lake earlier during the cross-country had left clothes and harness soaking wet, and therefore very slippery.

1–3. Coming in fast.

4. The rider should have had more weight distributed through her legs into the stirrups (compare Chris Collins 3).

5 and 6. Weight too far forward and short rein means that Aly is nearly pulled over her horse's head when Olivia blunders from the momentum of her big jump.

7. Lucky save.

Handicap of a long name. Lucinda Prior-Palmer after the dressage.

conditioned by the angle of the fence and by the number of paces needed for each approach. The rider should pace the course out very carefully, so that at the end of his inspection he knows his path as thoroughly as if it were marked out with white arrows on the turf.

There is not usually time during a one-day event to walk the cross-country more than once – twice at the most. Especially in cases where a novice horse and rider are involved, it is worth arriving at the event with plenty of time in hand for two walks around the course, one for first impressions and to get an idea of where you will be going, and the other, if possible in the company of an expert, to study particular problems posed by the course. Courses often appear less intimidating on second inspection.

Jumps such as the inevitable water-jump are worth especial attention. It is not safe to assume that the bottom of a stream may be solid throughout or that the depth of the water is constant; better to wade through it and be sure of the best line through. Alternative approaches should be considered – if, for instance, there is an obvious best way through the water and you are one of the last to compete, other competitors may have used this route so often that what was at the time of first examination a solid, shallow landing has become a hole dug by many hooves.

The same principle applies to soft patches in the ground, which may be quagmires after 50 horses have churned them up. At each of the fences that are not straightforward throughout their breadth alternative approaches must be worked out in case the original choice later becomes unjumpable. Finally, if the mount is a raw novice the route to choose is not the quickest but the easiest; ambition to win must be subjected to the long-term investment of a slow, safe, clear round which will leave the horse happy and confident.

After the rider has walked the course it is usually time for him to change into formal breeches and boots and ride the horse in for half-an-hour to an hour before the dressage test. When the test is over the horse may need to have boots fitted for the show jumping phase. After the show jumping his boots should be checked, his bandages, if worn, put on for the cross-country, and his rider must change from the show jumping jacket and cap into the cross-country sweater and crash helmet. When the cross-country phase is over, no matter how good a round has been jumped, the score will be invalidated in any competition where the standard is intermediate or higher if the rider forgets to unsaddle and weigh in.

At the end of the day, immediately following the cross-country, the horse's comfort is the first consideration. His saddle, boots and bandages should be removed and he should be washed from head to tail in lukewarm water, sweat-scraped and towelled to get most of the water off, and be examined for cuts or other forms of damage. Since he will not be thoroughly dried off he should be walked around until he is completely dry, wearing a sweat sheet and perhaps a blanket, depending on the heat of the day.

When the horse is dry, bandage his legs with gamgee and stable bandages as a comfort and support for tired legs and to keep him warm on the journey home. Cuts should be attended to from the first-aid box, a drink of 'chilled water' (hot water left to cool till lukewarm) offered, and without delay he should be loaded into the protective warmth and quiet of the horsebox, given praise, hay and a small feed. If possible you should drive home at the first opportunity, as the horse needs even more than his rider to get the journey over with and relax in his own home.

THREE-DAY EVENTS   Most three-day events involve at least five or six nights away from home – more if there is a very long journey or if one has to adapt to a change of climate. In most cases competitors take their own feed and hay along with them to avoid any possible upset caused by a change of diet. The five official days of a three-day event will start, say, on a Wednesday with the briefing of competitors, the official inspection of the course and the preliminary veterinary inspection. On Thursday, when the event first opens to spectators, the dressage tests begin, usually continuing until late on Friday afternoon. Saturday is speed and endurance day; Sunday, after the mandatory veterinary inspection, is kept for show jumping, and on Sunday evening those who live near enough will start to box up and go home.

Relaxing the horse on first arrival: Most competitors arrive early in the afternoon of the day before the briefing. After establishing where the horse is to be stabled and unloading some or all of the luggage, the first priority is to get the horse to accept and settle into his new surroundings. Much depends upon the animal's temperament. Some may prefer an hour or two in their new stable, maybe left with a small feed or whatever is their routine for that particular time of day, and coming out for exercise later in the afternoon. Others – the more highly-strung – will need a greater knowledge of their overall surroundings before they will settle down. Either way, the amount of exercise given will probably be one-and-a-half to two hours at a ridden walk, relaxing on a loose rein while the horse looks around and adapts himself.

Walk the horse around the grandstand area of the event, especially in the vicinity of the dressage arena. Tents will be going up, traffic for trade stands will be on the move, and the sooner the horse can be induced to accept these exciting surroundings – or better still become slightly bored by them – the easier it will be later to get a good dressage performance out of it.

You should keep to normal feeding times and stable routine throughout the event, as this will help the horse to settle in. If the horse is a greedy type it is advisable, unless he is bedded on shavings, to put a muzzle on him or to spray his straw with disinfectant to discourage him from eating.

BADMINTON 1976
Chevrons

Mark Phillips on Favour

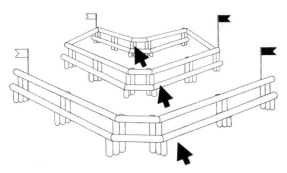

As can be seen from the plans above and overleaf, there are different ways to get through this maze. Many riders chose to go straight down the middle, though Mark Phillips said he instinctively felt that the best route through (arrowed) was to aim for the right-hand upright on the approach and to leave the Chevrons over the left. This gives him a fractionally longer stride between each element.

The rider has the mare balanced from leg to hand throughout, never for a moment losing his contact with her. Favour receives as much help as is possible in keeping her balance and her hocks under her.

Note the short, bouncy stride of the approach, precise and full of impulsion.

1

2

3

4

BADMINTON 1976
Chevrons

Joanna Winter on Stainless Steel

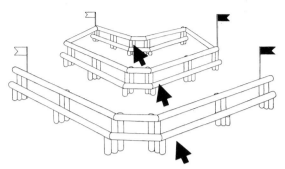

1

2

3

8

9

Coming in from the left the horse stops at the second element, swerving to the side that his rider would be least likely to expect. She is sitting well (3), and is therefore not seriously unbalanced.

A quick-thinking recovery (4, *et seq.*) is followed by good riding over an escape route made difficult by free-standing rails with no ground lines.

9. A fast exit turn. The rider is already looking ahead to the next fence.

Briefing of competitors: This, often the first official gathering of competitors (unless the veterinary inspection that is held before the start of each event precedes it), is usually a tense, though amusing, time for everyone. Because the end of months of training is now officially in sight it is no longer possible to pretend that today is just another day in a regular routine, and even the most experienced of riders will feel an extra surge of adrenalin when silence is called for and the director of the event starts to read out the rules. Friends may become adversaries during this lull before the storm, but it amounts to only a group of hard-fit riders getting instructions on what they will later have to perform, and nerves are quickly walked off during the following inspection of the course.

At the briefing the rider receives his number cloth, a plan of the course, and such official invitations as may be part of the entertainment side of the event.

Walking the course: The roads and tracks are usually driven after the briefing of competitors. Maybe eight miles of these, forming phase A and phase C of the speed and endurance test and divided by phase B, the steeplechase, will be gone over in party spirit directly after the briefing. Unless the competitor is riding a familiar course he should retrace the route later, making sure that he knows precisely where he must go and how much time is allowed for each phase. Given the distance, a knowledge of the terrain and of the natural speeds of his horse, he can then work out the exact times at which he should aim to pass selected points along the route. Without this time schedule he will not know on the day whether he is going too fast (no penalties, but tiring) or too slowly. Aim at arriving at the start of phases B and D with an extra two minutes in hand for checking such things as girths and boots.

Walking the steeplechase course should be done once or twice before the speed and endurance. The first walk, usually in the company of other competitors, sometimes gives little more than an impression of where one is going. Successive walks must establish where the marker flags are, how much riding is called for at each fence, the shortest route around the course and the speed at which one will have to travel to stay within the time allowed. The fences are usually so straightforward that the unwary rider may be trapped into underestimating the amount of wear and tear on the horse that is given a careless ride or is pushed too far inside the time allowed.

After phase C of the roads and tracks comes the ultimate test, the cross-country. This is the most important part of any event, and the course should be walked at least three times. The first walk is devoted to first impressions, which are invaluable because this is how the horse is later going to see it. Without examining the fences too closely, note the ones that are difficult to sight (such as a coffin). Establish the limits of the course, noting markers and where the course ropes will go up, and try to visualise how much narrower the course will be or will feel to be when crowds are leaning against the ropes. Penalty areas, clearly marked around each fence and usually also defined on the course plan, will show where it is safe to fall off without incurring penalties and where it is not. A thorough knowledge of the limits of penalty zones, reinforced during subsequent walks, may later help should a rider come unstuck without actually hitting the ground: he must know where to steer the horse, and for what distance, before he can safely let go without getting 60 penalty points clocked up against him. (Determined riders have been known to hang on upside down until they are outside the penalty zone.) But details of penalty areas can be worked out later; the first requirements are to understand how the horse will see it and to learn where one is going.

The second walk of three is usually the most time-consuming. An experienced rider/trainer/observer as companion for this walk can be a great help, pointing out details that the competitor may never have noticed. As Michael Moffett remarked on page 14, a problem unnoticed on foot may not exist as a problem when riding the course. The point of the second walk is to decide how and where each fence should be jumped, taking into account drops or landings into rising ground and how sharply the rider may have to pull back to make a turn. Is it better to take the difficult way across the corner of an angled combination, saving time but risking a run-out, or to go the slower way with a bounce in and out? What are the alternatives should the route you would prefer become unjumpable on the day because of damage done by earlier runners? Where should you kick on and where pull back and come in on a shortened stride – that is, which fences call for speed to clear a spread and which require discretion because of a combination or a punishing landing?

The hardest fences, idiosyncrasies of the course-builder aside, are usually the coffin and the water. The coffin, a post-and-rails followed by a concealed ditch in a gully followed by another post-and-rails, is a problem in unsighting because the approaching horse sees only the first and third elements of the combination. The ditch in the middle is visible only at the last minute, and therefore a horse going gaily into what he imagines is a straightforward double post-and-rails may register the downward drop too late and stop. Such fences should be approached on a very slow but bouncy stride, full of impulsion, so that the horse has time to see the ditch, recover from the unexpected shock of it, and still have enough time and impetus to jump. Coming in slowly but without impulsion, the horse may be able to manage the first and second elements of a coffin, but the jump out on uphill going is likely to be beyond his scope. Coming in fast, *if* the horse does not stop at the first element, will almost certainly land horse and rider in the ditch.

The water, usually a low approach jump into a dragging landing which could stop a galloping horse in its stride, calls for much the same respectful treatment. Give the horse as much time as possible on the approach, coming in slowly with enough impulsion so that he does not stop when he sees the water beyond the fence and lengthening

John Shedden, winner of the first Badminton of 1949.

1

5

4

RUSHALL 1975
Water Jump

Princess Anne on Mardi Gras

Typical mistake of a green horse, jumping far too big into water.

1. Having felt thrust of horse's fantastic launch, rider puts weight well back because the impact on landing is bound to be strong.

2. Impact with water unbalances horse. Rider's weight, which should have been distributed more through her knees, is on the balls of her feet. She is therefore...

3. *et seq.* – unseated.

93

Allow time for little things. Cleaning up will be necessary, even during competition.

fractionally in the last two or three strides so that the angle of landing is shallow and the horse is not stopped too drastically by contact with the water. The rider's weight should be well back on landing into water to encourage the horse to keep its balance and therefore its feet before it takes the next waterlogged stride forwards.

During the second walk around the cross-country (assuming that the rider has friends who are willing to help) decisions can be made on who will stand at which fence to see how the course is riding on the day and to report back to the rider just before he starts the course on where everyone is hitting the floor and where the course is riding smoothly.

The final walk of the course, usually done when the rider has completed his dressage test and has spent 24–48 hours chewing over the problems of his approach, is for confirmation. Walk directly around the course, on the exact route you intend to ride, so that precisely where you are going is clear in your mind. You should now know the course by heart and be in a position to gauge the amount of toll taken by the horse during the three preceding phases of the speed and endurance. It should thus be possible to know where you can start putting the pressure on the horse to get home within the allotted time.

Exercising the horse during the event is usually more a matter of brainwashing it than of keeping it fit. It should have arrived at the event in peak condition, probably ready to shy and spook at any excuse, and must stay at this peak of fitness if it is to run for its life during the cross-country. The usual difficulty is to get it to settle for its dressage test, and this is done more through psychology than by physically tiring it – it is anyway highly unlikely that you will be able to make a fit and supercharged horse physically tired, and is besides inadvisable.

Ride it for about two hours a day, lunging, schooling and hacking in the vicinity of the main arena so that the horse becomes used to the bustle of the trade stands and the mounting throngs of spectators. On the day before the dressage test an hour of gentle riding on the roads may help to settle it before serious schooling starts.

On the day before the cross-country the horse should have a short pipe-opener included in its exercise.

Preparing for the dressage test: On the day before the test, school the horse for perhaps an hour. Run through the movements of the test, choosing a random order so that the horse is not led to anticipate his movements during the test. If you have a dressage trainer he will be advising at this stage; if not, the criticism of any reliable ground jockey can be of great help.

Try to watch a few of the other competitors performing their tests in the arena (hard luck on those drawn early during the test days). If you can contrive to stand behind or beside the judges' position you will find out which parts of the test are not easily visible to them, and therefore will know where, with reasonable safety, you will later be able to cover up your or your horse's mistakes.

You will, of course, know the test by heart long before arriving at the event. Nonetheless it is prudent to read it over carefully the night before the test. A careless mistake in direction, speed or movement is expensive in points.

On the day of the test first settle the horse with steady exercise, walking and schooling until it relaxes. Ride the horse in for some time before the test – the length of time varies with each horse – working if possible under the guidance of your trainer.

Preparing for the speed and endurance test: On the morning of the cross-country, after his normal breakfast feed and stable routine, the horse may profit from being led out for half an hour and allowed to pick grass. The rest of the morning should be spent in the stable, left as undisturbed as possible. If he is drawn to run late in the day a small lunchtime feed may be given. Water should be taken away two hours before the start, food four hours before the start, and the horse should be left muzzled if he is bedded on straw in case he eats it and thereby thickens up his wind.

The rider should have his times worked out for all phases of the speed and endurance. Times of the start and finish of each phase should be clearly written on paper, sellotaped to the arm over the sleeve of the sweater, and covered with clear plastic to guard against rain and the splash of the water jump. Two watches are needed, one a normal one to show the time of day and the other a stop-watch for the precise duration of each phase. The better stop-watches show not only how many minutes have passed but, on a separate dial, how many minutes remain. If the watch is strapped to the bridge between the thumb and forefinger and the times are taped to the upper face of the arm above the wrist, the rider will not have to turn his hands when riding to check how he is getting on. A quick glance down rather than a movement of the hand or arm can, especially during the steeplechase and cross-country, save time and trouble. The stop-watch is, of course, strapped on over the gloves, which should be made of string with rubber finger-grips for maximum grip (leather slips when wetted by sweat or water). Shoulder straps on the rider's number-cloth should be pinned down to prevent slipping and pinioning the arms.

If the horse is not a nervous type, walking around for 15 or 20 minutes before the start of phase A is enough. If it is likely to take a hold during phase A and waste a lot of energy fighting you, canter it in circles in a quiet rhythm until it settles down. Come to the starting point, weighed out, saddled and ready to go, five minutes before the off, and walk the horse in circles until it is time to go.

After the cross-country immediately lead the horse back to the stables. Make much of him – even if his performance was by and large disastrous much of it may not have been his fault. Remove

Abundant equipment is vital: if you've left it at home it won't help you here.

his boots and bandages, wash him down thoroughly in luke-warm water, scrape and towel him and walk him around until he is dry and has stopped blowing. Return him to the stable, remove the studs from his shoes, inspect him for cuts and bruises and medicate as necessary. Rug up. Offer water with the chill off, at first just a couple of mouthfuls. Apply hot kaolin to all four legs from the hooves up to the hocks or knees and bandage over thickly to keep in the heat. Leave him with a little hay and more tepid water. When the stable yard is quiet and the cars outside have disappeared, lead the horse out for a short walk and pick, trotting a few paces to see that he is sound. If he is all right leave him in peace with his evening feed and hay.

After such a gruelling day the horse is almost certain to be stiff, and may also have incurred some cuts and knocks. No effort must be spared to help him to pass the veterinary inspection on the following morning and to be supple enough to complete the show-jumping phase. Packing his hooves with cow dung mixed with clay can help to ease jarred-up feet; hot kaolin poultices left on overnight will take much of the strain from his legs; Faradism treatment, a kind of electric vibrator best operated by a qualified physiotherapist or other expert, will help to relax the muscles of a stiff back and may need to be applied both in the evening and again the following morning. Other comforts, depending on the type and temperament of the horse, may be administered as necessary, not forgetting that his overwhelming need is likely to be for rest and quiet.

Preparation for the final veterinary inspection begins with an early morning examination of the horse. Trot him out first thing to see that he is sound. Leave him, still kaolin-poulticed, to enjoy his breakfast feed, returning with plenty of time in hand to groom him thoroughly and get the sticky kaolin off his legs. Three-quarters of an hour before the appointment comes up for your veterinary inspection take the horse out for a half-hour ridden walk or lunge, with maybe a sharp trot or canter to loosen him up. Get a friend to keep you informed on the progress of the inspection so that you can arrive in plenty of time but without so much in hand that your horse has to hang around unduly while he is waiting. Brush any traces of kaolin, which will show white as it dries, off his legs and oil his hooves before leading down to the inspection area.

At the veterinary inspection lead the horse round in the waiting area until only three horses are left to go before you are called. Take off the horse's rug and trot him up and back as a last-minute practice before he trots up and back for his inspection.

The old horse dealer's trick of holding a horse very close to the bit so that it appears to be pulling when in fact it would rather stop is unlikely to work before a panel of experienced veterinary surgeons. When the horse is called for, lead him up and get him to stand squarely while the examiners look for bumps and lumps and cuts,

Lucinda and Wide Awake passing the veterinary inspection – with judges French, Italian and American.

Richard Meade and Jacob Jones, also at Badminton 1976.

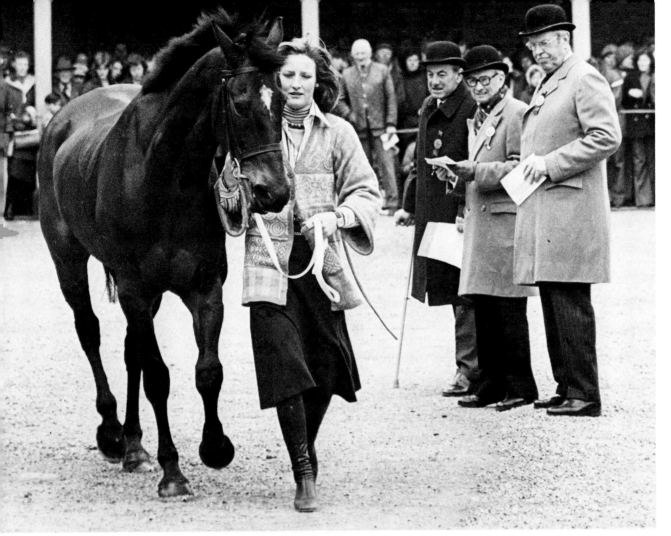

Princess Anne and Mark Phillips before the show-jumping.

OPPOSITE: A husband-and-wife team: with Goodwill at Tidworth, 1975.

BELOW: Windsor. Princess Anne bandaging up Arthur of Troy before going home.

then walk the horse away, turn, and trot back past the panel. A horse that is a borderline case can be covered up by a tight hold on the reins as he turns to trot back, causing him to tense up and perhaps dance or trot sideways so that a slight unevenness in his action is difficult to see – but, again, the examiners are usually wise to more tricks than the competitors know and any suspicious action will cause them to stop the horse, inspect it very carefully, and send it up again ordering a 'loose rein'.

After the inspection lead the horse straight back to his stable, leave him some hay to pick (enough to keep him occupied, but not a bellyful), and give him his lunchtime feed at about 11.30.

Walking the show-jumping course is usually done after the veterinary inspection. Since it is intended only as a test of obedience to ensure that the horse is still willing to perform for his rider after a hard endurance day, the problems of a pure show jumping course will be absent. None of the fences will be big, and the tricks and traps of difficult stridings and of fences at odd angles will not be encountered, though special thought should be given to the strides between the elements of the combination fences. Look for sharp turns, and establish the line you will take between each fence. Discover the best place to turn in for each obstacle.

When you have decided how to ride the course walk the course again, as in the cross-country, to be sure of your line.

Riding the horse in for the show jumping, depending on its degree of stiffness, may take up to an hour. Begin by suppling him up with dressage and follow with plenty of small pop-jumps and spreads. Though he is almost certain to be stiff, tactfully and firmly urge him to use every muscle in his body until he is loose enough all over to jump a round of fences, all under four feet high, to the best of his ability. Feeling sorry for the horse at this stage is misguided sympathy: no matter how brilliant an effort he may have made on the day before he has not proved himself as a three-day event horse until he has cleared the simple show-jumps, and the rider's task must be to iron out the knots in the horse's body and get him free, concentrating and obedient enough to jump slowly and accurately. He has to be made to understand that he is no longer jumping fast and fairly flat, as he was during the cross-country phase, but with suppleness and a rounded back.

Riding the horse in will be interrupted for the parade in the arena of all competitors still in at this stage. Coming out before a massed crowd, bands playing, handkerchiefs waving and cameras clicking and flashing, makes a complete break in the horse's concentration. The rider of an excitable horse should be prepared to trot into the collecting ring and straight on into the arena at the last minute and to ride straight out again to a quieter place when the parade has finished.

Practice fences will have been set up near the collecting ring. The horse will need to know when he touches a fence, since he may have

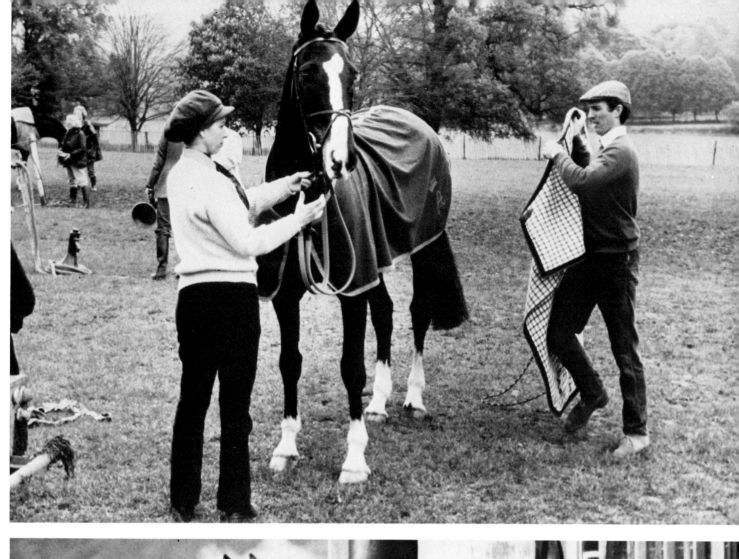

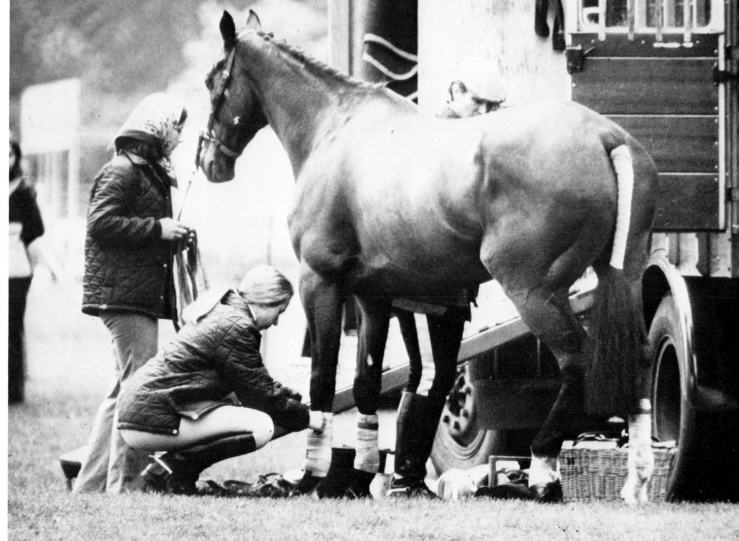

become accustomed to rattling the solid-built cross-country fences and could easily tip the precarious show jumping fences down if he cannot feel what he is doing, so you may now be riding without protective boots and bandages. Depending on the character of the horse, and on what the rider instinctively feels is best for him, he may be schooled at a canter while the rider's helpers lower a practice rail so close to the ground that it is little more than a stride-breaker; if permitted, trot over it a couple of times from both directions, and then canter in more circles while the pole is raised progressively up to a height of maybe four feet. Taking a spread jump a few times will open him out. When the horse is using himself and jumping well, dismount and lead him round until a few minutes before you are due in the ring. Just before your turn arrives to compete a jump or two over an upright at about four feet high may help to set him back on his hocks and enliven his concentration.

When the show jumping is over the horse should be taken straight back to the stable. If he has sweated up – as he probably will – wash him down again, dry him, rug up and bandage, offer him water with the chill off and attend to any cuts and knocks that may still need easing after the cross-country day. Make sure he is thoroughly warm and happy. If he is to be taken home that night, give him a small feed and an hour or two of peace before loading him into the horsebox.

On arriving home trot the horse up to check that he is sound. If no medicaments need be applied, feed him a bran mash, hay up, and leave him alone to rest. As long as he is reasonably clean, well bandaged, rugged and warm he is better left to sleep it off by himself.

The following morning trot the horse up again to check for soundness. He can now be cleaned and groomed thoroughly. If the weather is suitable, turn him out in the field for an hour.

IN ACTION

Dressage

The object of dressage is to demonstrate the harmonious development of the horse and its perfect understanding with its rider. As opposed to the High School Airs above the Ground, which consist mostly of unnatural movements designed to protect the rider in a battle (such as training the horse to leap vertically to a height from which its rider can stab the enemy), the movements of dressage are all natural to the horse and can be seen over a period of time in any field where several horses are turned out together. The *piaffe*, for example, in which the horse dances on the spot, is part of the normal introductory routine of horse to horse. But such movements as this are confined to advanced dressage competitions and are not included in the simple exercises of the three-day event test.

The event rider is not expected to demonstrate as high a degree of skill in dressage as the pure dressage rider. Nor should he be: training a horse to anywhere near top dressage standard takes a minimum of four years' exclusive concentration, and the event rider has other skills to develop simultaneously. Three-day event dressage is thus comparatively elementary, effective more as a demonstration of obedience, control and horsemanship than one of a high form of art. Judges look to see that the horse is at all times on the bit, full of impulsion, going softly but energetically, responsive, and always moving straight (maintaining the latter is a lot more difficult than it sounds).

The most difficult factor facing the event rider is that, while the pure dressage horse is trained for dressage only and may therefore be comparatively physically soft and mentally docile, the event horse is corned up to a peak of fitness for the second day's cross-country and will probably be hard to discipline, especially when it is excited by the crowd.

Having ridden the horse in thoroughly before the test, the rider may choose to enter the dressage ring on a loose rein so that the horse can look around him and take in his surroundings before he is brought back under strict control. Some horses, though, are far too much excited by the atmosphere, and with such animals the rider is wiser to keep his horse's attention concentrated only on the job in hand.

1. Richard Meade on Jacob Jones, Badminton 1976.

2. Bruce Davidson and Irish Cap, at the World Championships 1974. A very similar position to Phillips's, though Irish Cap is seen here more strung out than Columbus and therefore looking uglier.

3. Mark Phillips and Columbus, also at the World Championships. The horse is the wrong shape for dressage, difficult to get up together without becoming overbent (that is, the line of the face falls behind the vertical).

4. World Championship leader after the dressage phase, Russia's V. Laniugin riding Tost. Note the unusual riding style: straight line from shoulder to wrist, rigidity of hands, seeming lack of depth of seat.

When riding the horse in aim to get him going well but a little dully while he is still outside the main performance area. The little bit extra that will make his performance come alive will be added when he comes into the big arena, is surrounded by grandstands, strange people and unfamiliar noises, followed by the hush that falls when the bell goes for him to commence his test.

The rhythm of the test must be always in the forefront of the rider's mind. The whole test should be performed in the same flowing, easy rhythm, no matter what paces are being demonstrated. Harmony can be shown by a continuous motion, like a sea lapping away at the quayside, and even the halts and immobilities become part of the metronomic flow. Don't let this feeling become misinterpreted into a dull, lifeless test – there must be fire for the movements to have brilliance.

Having already worked out the judges' angle on the test, the rider will know where he can, if he must, best cover up mistakes by himself or his horse. But if one movement is a failure it should not be allowed to affect the rest of the performance. The mistake, once made, is behind you: now do your best to perfect the remaining movements.

Always try to be precisely accurate. Aiming to do each movement just a fraction before the appropriate marker will usually put the rider exactly on target. Accuracy is judged by the relation of the rider's body to the marker, not by the line of the front or back end of the horse. Riding well into the corners will help the rider get or maintain his horse on the bit, and may also help convince the judges that the horse is well-schooled.

Canter serpentines should be ridden so that the horse is broadside on to the judges at the moment of crossing the centre line. This helps to prevent the rider making points of his turns instead of curves – points will be so sharp that they will encourage the horse to change legs when he should be executing a counter-canter. The serpentine movement should be made with flowing, rounded turns, not sharp or angular ones.

If the rider uses his voice when he is schooling at home, which he probably does, he will find he can continue to use this aid during his test. If he is careful to keep his voice down so that the judges

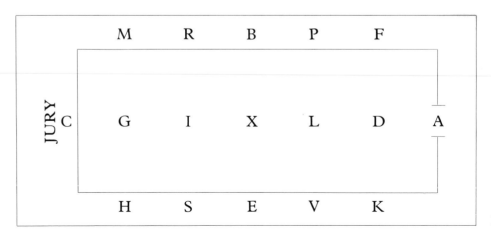

Plan of dressage arena.

F.E.I. THREE-DAY EVENT DRESSAGE TEST (1975)

		TEST	MAXIMUM MARKS
1	A	Enter at working canter	6
	X	Halt – Immobility – Salute – Proceed at working trot	
2	C	Track to the left	
	S	Medium trot	6
	EBE	Circle to the left 20 metres diameter	
	EV	Medium trot	
3	V	Working trot	
	A	Down centre line	6
	L	Circle to the left 10 metres diameter	
4	LS	Half-pass (left)	6
5	C	Halt – Rein back 5 steps – Proceed at working trot without halting	6
6	R	Medium trot	
	BEB	Circle to the right 20 metres diameter	6
	BP	Medium trot	
7	P	Working trot	
	A	Down centre line	6
	L	Circle to the right 10 metres diameter	
8	LR	Half-pass (right)	6
9	C	Halt – Immobility 5 seconds – Proceed at working trot	6
10	HXF	Change rein at extended trot (rising)	6
	F	Working trot	
11	KXM	Change rein at extended trot	6
	M	Working trot	
12	C	Medium walk	
	HSXPF	Extended walk	6
	F	Medium walk	
13	A	Working canter – Circle to the right 10 metres diameter	6
14	AC	Serpentine 3 loops, the first and the third true canter, the second counter-canter	6
15	MXK	Change rein at extended canter	6
	K	Working trot	
16	A	Working canter – Circle to the left 10 metres diameter	6
17	AC	Serpentine 3 loops, the first and the third true canter, the second counter-canter	6
18	HXF	Change rein at extended canter	6
	F	Working trot	
19	A	Down centre line	6
	L	Working canter to the right	
20	G	Halt – Immobility – Salute	6
		Leave arena at walk on a long rein TOTAL	120

Collective marks:

1. Paces (freedom and regularity)	6
2. Impulsion (desire to move forward, elasticity of the steps and engagement of the hind quarters)	6
3. Submission (attention and obedience, lightness and freedom of the movements, acceptance of the bit)	6
4. Position, seat of the rider, correct use of the aids	6
	144

cannot hear him and is able to speak to his horse without obviously moving his lips, use of the voice will be a considerable help.

The F.E.I. three-day event dressage test (advanced level) varies slightly once every few years, though its essentials are much the same, and the 1975 test on page 105 is liable to remain unaltered for several years:

Marking Each of the 20 movements in the test and of the 4 sets of collective marks is awarded from 0 to 6 good marks by each of the three judges. There are therefore 144 good marks which can be awarded by each judge.

Any penalties incurred for overtime or errors of course are deducted from each judge's sheet and the total marks of the three judges are then averaged. The good marks thus obtained are subtracted from 144 to express the score in penalty points.

Time The time allowed for the test is $7\frac{1}{2}$ minutes, measured from the exact moment, after the salute to the judges, when the horse moves forward, until the horse is brought to a standstill at the end of the test and the rider salutes the judges once more. Time faults are incurred at the rate of half a mark for every second taken over $7\frac{1}{2}$ minutes.

Errors of Course The test must be executed from memory. Errors of course or wrong sequence of movements, whether corrected or not, are penalised as follows:

First error	2 marks
Second error	5 marks
Third error	8 marks
Fourth error	Elimination

Roads and Tracks, Steeplechase

Times of phases A, B, and C will have been worked out in advance and taped securely to the rider's arm. Kilometre markers along the route will help the rider to check his time as he passes.

Come into the start as quietly as possible and ride phase A with utmost sympathy and tact, trying always to save the horse unnecessary exertion and to keep him to the best and most level ground. The official object of phase A is simply to complete the distance within the given time, but the rider's unofficial objective will also be to save his horse as much as he can for the cross-country. Depending on the preference of the horse, the roads and tracks can be taken at a steady trot nearly all the way or can be divided into periods of cantering and walking. Some riders like to open their horse up for a short gallop on any appropriate going during phase A, so that he will blow away the cobwebs of the previous night before he has to do his two-mile steeplechase.

Penalty points are awarded for each second in excess of the time allowed, but no bonuses are given for finishing inside the time. Nonetheless, since phase B follows directly upon phase A, time your arrival at the start of the steeplechase course to allow one-and-a-half to two minutes in hand so that girths can be tightened and any emergency repairs carried out. Since there will not be time for the rider to dismount and perform these checks himself, and since he will anyway probably need the time for such things as resetting his stop-watch, try to arrange for someone to be on hand to help with the horse. Spare tack, as suggested in the following cross-country section, should always be available. Except for international competitions, when private vehicles are not allowed on the course but organised transport is normally provided, spares are usually carried in the boot of the car to the start of phase B and thence to the start of phase D.

The steeplechase should be ridden at around 26 m.p.h. Jump off fast and set a good pace for the first two fences, keeping the horse moving along at a fair pace but still on the bit. He should already

Mark Phillips and Brazil
on the roads and tracks.

have been taught to jump at speed without checking his stride, and if this has not been done he will lose valuable time by checking before each fence and will also take more out of himself by the constant breaks in rhythm.

More bad riding takes place on the steeplechase course than in any other part of a three-day event. Letting the horse lose his stride, become unbalanced, or positioning the rider's weight so that the horse has to take most of it will take more out of the horse than he can afford with the taxing cross-country yet to come.

The time at the end of phase B, no matter how fast or slowly the horse has gone, is taken simultaneously with the start of phase C. Let the horse unwind his gallop as he comes into phase C, so that

Barbara Hammond and Red Rusky take a steeplechase fence.

maybe by the time he has slowed to a walk he will already have covered half a kilometre of the second phase of the roads and tracks. Allow him to walk for as long as possible, always keeping in mind the time allowance for phase C, until he has recovered the best part of his breath; but beware of walking for more than four or five minutes because you may later have to move faster than is desirable to catch up on the time.

Phase C should be ridden even more considerately than phase A. The longer the distance of this phase the better for the horse, as it gives him more time to recover from phase B before the cross-country.

Aim to arrive at the Box for the start of the cross-country two minutes before the official end of phase C; that is, with 12 minutes in hand in the Box instead of the statutory 10. The extra two minutes' rest will be of much value to the horse, and will give him a good deal more in hand for the cross-country.

Come into the Box at a trot, so that the examining panel can see that the horse is moving straight and sound. Slip off the horse as soon as you arrive and be prepared to answer any questions from the veterinary surgeons. In all likelihood, if the horse has trotted in sound and looking happy there will be no hold up and the rider will be free to get on with the task of readying his horse for the cross-country.

IN ACTION

The Cross-Country

The official ten minutes in the Box before the start of phase D (12 minutes if the rider has timed it cleverly) are the most hectic time of the whole three-day event and require the most organisation. The objects of the break are to permit an official examination of the horse to ensure that he is fit to continue and to refresh and if necessary re-kit the horse for the cross-country.

In order to achieve this with any guarantee of efficiency the competitor must arrange to have, in his preordained place in the Box, at least the following tools and spares:

spare set of horseshoes with studs
spare saddle and numnah
assorted spare parts of tack (stirrups and leathers, breastplate, spurs, reins with rubber handparts, girths, headcollar, etc)
first aid kit
3-gallon container of warm water, stoppered
rubber bucket
sponge for washing horse
scraper
assorted towels
sweat rug
travelling blanket
large tin of soft paraffin or vaseline
rubber gloves
spare overreach boots
spare support boots and bandages
hoofpick
plastic container of water for washing out the horse's mouth
sponge for washing out the horse's mouth
drink for rider (glucose or lemonade)
spare clothing for the rider and a jacket to keep him warm on a cold day

Unless this small mountain of spare parts is automatically on hand sooner or later a time will come when some small fraction of the whole, such as a snapped stirrup leather, cannot be replaced when it is urgently needed and the whole effort of the event will become fruitless. The pile of stable equipment is needed for the task of

OPPOSITE: A steady, relentless canter should be maintained throughout. Otherwise . . .

washing down and drying off the horse, which is done immediately the animal has been passed by the inspection committee. Three competent and well-briefed assistants should be on hand to help.

OPPOSITE: The going may have changed since the rider walked the course.

As the rider trots in and dismounts one of his helpers should have the rubber bucket ready, filled with warm water. The horse is unsaddled at once, and while the rider sets about acquiring information about the course the horse is led to his corner, washed from head to tail and scraped and towelled dry with one person working on each side of the horse simultaneously. The third person holds the horse's head, and unless the horse is extremely docile or stoic the holder should be a strong man because the horse will probably be fussing and fidgeting around and may be hard to persuade to stand still. Many people like to precede the washing operation by tying towels around the top of each of the horse's legs to prevent his boots and bandages from getting wet, but this is not always thought necessary, as the amount of water that will run down as far as the lower legs is minimal and anyway the horse will soon be jumping through water.

When the horse has been towelled off a sweat rug is thrown over him. Pick out his feet and check that the shoes are all right and the studs still in place. Examine and treat minor cuts from the first-aid box. Two helpers, now wearing rubber gloves, should grease his legs thickly down the front, plastering vaseline (soft white paraffin) down all four legs from body to hoof over boots and bandages and all. The value of this thick greasing operation has been proved on many occasions – if the horse just hits the top of a solid fence he may thus be enabled to slide over it instead of being held back by the drag of dry legs.

Wash the horse's mouth out thoroughly with a spongeful of water, and walk him round to dry off. If it is cold, throw the stable blanket over him to keep his loins warm. Meanwhile someone should check that the selection committee do not want to have another look at the horse. Three or four minutes before it is time to start, call in the horse and saddle up.

The rider, meanwhile, if lucky with his helpers, has been able to escape from most of the work, except for such supervision as he feels obliged to perform, and concentrate on acquiring information about how the coming course is riding. His fence inspectors, stationed at the fences he particularly wants to know about, will tell him how things are going in their areas, and there will usually be some other expert around to tell him how the course is riding as a whole. Closed-circuit television, often available, can be another great help. The rider should keep himself warm and drink a small glass of whatever energy-producing beverage he has chosen to have on hand.

About two minutes from the off the rider should remount and tighten the girths from above. By this time the horse should have stopped blowing and be moving only lightly under the ribs. Just before the start, having listened to the Starter calling out the count-down, come up into the small starting box.

THE GALLOP

Princess Anne on Mardi Gras
Janet Hodgson on Larkspur

Considerate riding saves the horse between fences.
1 and 2: Janet Hodgson and Larkspur. Princess
Anne's position (3 and 4) is particularly good, weight
poised over the centre of Mardi Gras's gravity and
body streamlined for the line of least resistance to
the wind.

1

2

3

4

The rest depends on luck, your horse and on the experience of the rider. Stick to your original riding plan, using alternative approaches only at fences where you know from what you have learned in the Box that your preferred route has become unadvisable or unjumpable. A strong, relentless canter should be established and maintained as much as is possible, since every break in the horse's rhythm loses precious time in getting going again. Hindsight will tell you if you have gone too fast or too slowly early on, finishing with not enough left to come home cleanly, or with a clear round, a lot in hand, and unnecessary time penalties. Hindsight accumulates into experience, and the cooler the rider's head the more quickly will this experience be gained.

Falls and refusals should be accepted philosophically and without panic. In the event of a fall or refusal, help from a friend or casual spectator is forbidden except when catching a loose horse and helping the rider to remount or adjust his saddlery. The hot blood of the chase, knowing that you may be gaining on the horse in front and are being pursued by the horse behind, adds zest and courage to what is for many the finest of all possible cross-country rides.

It is perfectly acceptable, though uncomfortable, to slip up or fall on the flat provided one is outside the penalty zone surrounding each obstacle. Penalties, which are added to any time faults incurred, are usually as follows:

First refusal, run-out or circle of horse at an obstacle: 20 penalties.
Second refusal, run-out or circle at same obstacle: 40 penalties.
Third refusal, run-out or circle at same obstacle: elimination.
Fall of horse and/or rider at obstacle: 60 penalties (that is why one tries to hang on until outside the penalty zone).
Second fall of horse and/or rider at obstacles during the steeple-chase phase: elimination.
Third fall of horse and/or rider at obstacles during the cross-country: elimination.
Omission of obstacle or passing on the wrong side of a flag: elimination.
Retaking an obstacle already jumped: elimination.
Jumping obstacles in the wrong order: elimination.

The scoring is entirely on a penalty basis. No bonuses are given for completing the course inside the time. When the rider reaches the end of the cross-country he must unsaddle and weigh in. If he is below the weight he may include the horse's bridle, but if he is still underweight he will be eliminated. Dismounting and unsaddling must take place in the unsaddling enclosure in front of the steward responsible for the weighing, and at his order (dismounting before the steward requests it is improper).

The following pages illustrate some of the many different types of obstacle that may be encountered on the cross-country. Caption comments are intended to point up what may have gone right or wrong, but no claims are made to infallibility.

LOCKO PARK, DERBYSHIRE 1975

Janet Hodgson on Gretna Green

A slight dip in the ground a stride or two before the fence produced this interesting sequence, where it would seem that Gretna Green is not collecting herself up sufficiently to produce the magnificent leap she makes. In frame 6 the rider rightly allows her weight to come back, as a peck on landing would be a possibility after such a big jump; but (7) the mare pulls away easily. Note the rider's hands: the horse has complete freedom throughout, though contact is well maintained.

I

Janet Hodgson's comments:

'Gretna Green is the sort of horse who sets herself right.'

1. 'Rather than looking at the fence she's getting herself together.'

2. 'Still sorting herself out.'

3. 'She always jumps very big anyway.'

4. 'Absolutely extraordinary how far she's got her hind legs under her from the preceding frame.'

BADMINTON 1976
Luckington Lane

Lucinda Prior-Palmer on Wide Awake

A bold horse going gaily and jumping big.
Note alertness of ears and eyes, the horse's
continual concentration on the jump ahead of him.

The movement of the hind legs in frames 6, 7, 8
and 9 is unusually great. In frame 7 the horse's
hooves are tucked so far under his belly that they
are almost under his rider's feet. Notice how far
across the bank this takes him until he finally
touches down for his next take-off (9).

Rider's contact and weight distribution are good,
though in frame 4 her hands are too high.

BADMINTON 1976
Double Ski Jump

Robert Desourdy on George

Compare this sequence with the sequence overleaf. Here, the horse is more experienced than the rider. On pages 122–3 the rider is more experienced than the horse.

1–3. The horse never looks like stopping, but lowers himself carefully over the drop with good concentration. The rider's weight is correctly positioned, and (3) he slips his reins nicely.

But (4, 5) he fails to pick up the reins in time and approaches the next element out of contact with his horse.

6–7. The rider's contact through his seat has completely gone. He is now sitting 'above' his horse, and has no grip through the knees or thighs. He saves himself on landing by screwing his body to the angle of the horse. Had the horse blundered, he would have been in no position to help.

BADMINTON 1976
Double Ski Jump

Richard Meade on Jacob Jones

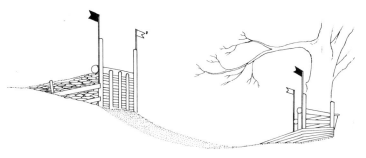

1

2

Here, the rider governs throughout.

1. Coming into the first element with a strong, deep seat.

2. The horse would like to stop, but the rider pushes on hard with seat and whip while maintaining contact with the horse's mouth.

3, 4. A big, rather nervous jump out. The rider slips his reins and sits back, prepared for (5) the slight blunder on landing.

6. He picks up his reins fast and rebalances the horse, pushing on with his seat (7, 8) into a perfect, controlled jump.

9. An exemplary show of balance and control.

7

8

9

TIDWORTH 1975
Bourne Ford and Rails

Mary Gordon-Watson on Highness

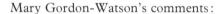

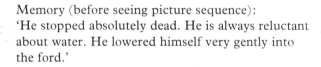

Mary Gordon-Watson's comments:

Memory (before seeing picture sequence):
'He stopped absolutely dead. He is always reluctant
about water. He lowered himself very gently into
the ford.'

On seeing the pictures she said she felt that the
stop (frames 4 and 5) should have been counted as a
refusal. 'If the horse loses his forward momentum –
especially if a *back* leg goes back – it's counted as a
stop.'

6. 'He walked all over the fence. Not exactly
copybook style.

'If the horse isn't very bold you don't want to go
into water too fast because it stops him. I
approached that fence rather faster than I normally
would because I knew Highness would slow up
before he got to it. But I didn't think he would
slow up *that* much!'

General Comment:

Highness doesn't want to go, and makes it clear. Mary pushes and encourages him on throughout.

6, 7, 8. Rather than jump in, Highness just lowers himself into the water. Very sensible.

11, 12. He stands off a long way at the rails, which leaves Mary slightly behind. She gives him the freedom he needs with length of rein, and helps as much as possible with the distribution of her weight.

TIDWORTH 1975
Bourne Ford and Rails

Sue Hatherly on Maribou

Sue Hatherly's comments:

1, 2. 'I was coming in a bit too fast.'

3. 'Doesn't it look as if he's going to hit that water and we won't be able to avoid a disaster? Either I'm going to fall off as he comes to a sudden halt, or he's going to peck on landing.'

4, 5. 'I haven't given him an extra inch of rein – I never do.'

6. 'Didn't he pick up well?'

10

11

General Comment:

1–3. A beautifully controlled but bold jump in.

4. Such good balance from horse and rider that Maribou doesn't flounder despite the over-knee depth of the water. Sue could have been more upright in her body to give even more security should the horse have pecked, but contact with seat and legs is close throughout.

7–11. A strong exit. The horse goes boldly away. The rider's contact never changes during this excellent performance. The horse is always in her hand, and she is thus really helping him to collect himself together.

RIGHT: Where it all begins, and, BELOW, often ends.

OPPOSITE PAGE:
LEFT: A time keeper at Bramham.
RIGHT: Bramham again – a mixed bag of spectators.
BELOW: Grooms, like horses, get wet and bored.

129

LIPHOOK 1975
Rails and Brook Jump

Lucinda Prior-Palmer on Be Fair
Mark Phillips on Persian Holiday

The two horses shown here are unlike in build and experience. Be Fair (ABOVE) is more compact and catlike in his movements than the bigger, rangier Persian Holiday, who is four years his junior.

Yet the photographs on this page show very similar approaches. Both horses look well down into the drop as they go through and both crouch and lower themselves carefully, though Be Fair's forward momentum is greater, his hocks tucked more tightly under him and his belly lowered closer to the ground.

The positions of the riders are also remarkably alike, with only Mark's downward glance and Lucinda's onward one to suggest the difference in their horses' experience.

ABOVE and BELOW the positions of the riders give
more indication of their mounts, as Mark sits well
back and slips his reins while Lucinda merely shifts
her weight.
Going on through the water, the faster, more
compact movements of Be Fair become more
evident.

CHATSWORTH 1975
Sunken Road

Rachel Bayliss on Gurgle the Greek

Rachel Bayliss's comments:

Memory (before seeing picture sequence): 'A mini-disaster. He had started off hopping round the course very beautifully. Normally at a fence like this I'd pull him right back to a slow canter and then he'd just pop over and leave me lots of room. Either I got there without being confident of getting up the steps, or he jumped in too big and then there was no room before we went up.'

On seeing the pictures:

1 and 2. 'I'm sure he'll land too far out and not have enough room.'

4 and 5. 'He got a stride – isn't it peculiar? – and then he sort of landed in a heap. It felt very heapish to me.'

6, 7, 8. 'I thought, "Sit tight and pray." *He* seemed to know all about it, but I'd lost him completely. I wish there hadn't been another step up.'

9, 10, 11. 'I didn't think I'd landed near enough to get up the next step. He's very clever. I think it's remarkable that he made it at all.'

General Comment:

The horse is given all the freedom he needs. The rider is right with him and is not getting left behind or jerked on in front.

1–3. Nice, collected short jump into the lane.

5. Rider sits deep and strong and keeps contact with her hands.

7. Gurgle only just gets up on the step. The distance between the first element and the bank was awkward for a long-striding horse.

8, 9. One back leg never makes it. However, the horse still rises immediately for the final element off the power of one hind leg and both his shoulders. People forget sometimes how important the shoulder and forearm thrust is to enable a horse to jump.

10

11

CHATSWORTH 1975
Sunken Road

Michael Moffett on Demerara

Michael Moffett's comments:

Memory: 'I was trying to open up a stride a bit going down into the dip. I think I went right and left to give Demerara more room so that he didn't have to lose a stride.'

On seeing the pictures:
3, 4. 'Going quite strong. A good long stride in there will probably put him just right. Yes, he's done a longer stride in the bottom, which will give me more room on the way up.'

5–8. 'I'm left behind.'

9. 'He's going to cut that corner again. He's going to get that photographer.'

General Comment:

Michael's style is that little bit more behind the horse's movement than Rachel's. This is not a mistake, but a mannerism often adopted by riders who have ridden refusers and so have learned to sit behind the horse (NB: Demerara is not an example of this sort of horse).

1–4. Similar good, short, balanced jump to Rachel's.

9

6. Note how athletically the hind legs snap up.

5–8. Elbows stuck well out. Not a fault, but a means of maintaining contact with the horse's mouth when the neck draws back on take-off.

BURGHLEY 1975
Trout Hatchery

Richard Meade on Tommy Buck

1. Apparently a perfect approach. The horse is jumping with confidence, and the rider appears to feel that all is going well. But . . .

2. Tommy Buck seems to have lost his hindlegs and just gets his front end over. He is straddled on the bar.

3. Most horses caught in position 2 would have stopped and drawn back. With great courage, helped by a boost from the reverberating bar above the log and by persuasion from his jockey, Tommy Buck drags his back end after him into the water. The rider throws his weight back to help the horse on landing. Note Richard's strong leg position, which hardly alters throughout, and good distribution of weight through the knees into the feet.

4. The rider is thrown forward by the impact as the horse catches his hind legs on the bar, but the position of his seat and legs is still strong.

5. Beginning to pick up the reins.

6. A quick recovery. The horse is back and balanced and going again, and the rider's contact is strong and sure.

7. An excellent jump out. The horse is happy and confident and the rider totally in command.

BURGHLEY 1975
Trout Hatchery

Princess Anne on Goodwill

This series of photographs shows a superb recovery by horse and rider due to an unusual feat of balance.

1. On the downhill approach into the jump the horse is not sufficiently back on his hocks. The rider's weight is a little forward, but she is apparently not expecting a stop and is driving on with her legs.

2. Goodwill drops a foreleg on the rail, an unusual situation which could possibly have been caused by a slip on take-off. Feeling the impact, Princess Anne slips her reins and begins to move her weight backwards.

3. Goodwill has got his foreleg free and is attempting a fast 'save', but the impact has turned his whole body sideways. His rider's immediate backward move to keep her weight as much as possible off the front of her unbalanced mount is a fine acrobatic feat.

I

2

3

4. Horse and rider are trying with everything they have to regain balance, but a plunge into the water seems at this stage unavoidable.

5. The beginnings of recovery: the horse has got his body straight, but has momentarily lost his hindlegs through the impact with the water. The rider is trying to get her weight back over the centre of gravity of her horse.

6. The amazing recovery momentarily leaves both unbalanced. Princess Anne's position here is highly precarious, but . . .

7. Very quickly she picks up her reins and moves her weight forward. Horse and rider are now going nicely away from what seemed certain disaster.

ABOVE: Spectators at Windsor, watching the Dressage.

RIGHT: From Windsor you can see the show jumping from the tea tent. These two connoisseurs regularly attend both eventing and horse racing in Britain.

Show Jumping

As has already been said, this is not a test of the horse's jumping ability but a test of his obedience and willingness to continue. It has become also a test of the level-headedness of the rider, since the strain of being in the lead with 'one fence in hand' or of needing only a steady clear to win, plus the electric excitement of the crowd, can easily result in unnecessary errors of judgment. Having got this far, with good performances in dressage and speed and endurance, it is easy to throw it all away because of tension. In fact, if the horse has been properly suppled up and the rider remains calm and confident despite the atmosphere, all that is needed is a round that you know very well is so easily within your abilities that you would think nothing of it under any other circumstances.

Again, the official time allowed for the course does not allow for bonus points but only for penalties in excess of the allotted time. Other penalties are as follows:

First refusal, run-out or circle before an obstacle: 10 penalties.
Second disobedience in the whole test: 20 penalties.
Third disobedience in the whole test: elimination.
Knocking down a fence (rapping does not count if the fence stays up): 10 penalties.
Landing on the boundary of the water, or in the water: 10 penalties.
Jumping a fence in the wrong order: elimination.
Taking the wrong course without going back and rectifying the mistake: elimination.
Fall of horse and/or rider: 30 penalties.
In show jumping, as in each phase of the speed and endurance test, there is a set time allowed for completing the course. Penalties are given for exceeding this time up to a maximum time limit. Exceeding the time limit in any section of the event results in elimination – so does weighing in afterwards at less than 165 lbs, so remember to carry the proper weight.

Don't be put off by professional show jumpers, who would consider three-day event show jumping laughably easy. Maybe, if they also had to ride the cross-country, the joke would be on them.

Bruce Davidson and Irish Cap, a perfect show jumping example. The rider never moves his hands, his back is neither straight nor stiff, he has a fine, deep seat, and his weight is evenly distributed down the knee and into the foot. It is all balanced and fluid.

Within a stride of landing, Davidson has Irish Cap under compact control, attention focussed on the next fence.

The Montreal Olympics

The 1976 Olympic Games was an unqualified triumph for American team trainer Jack Le Goff. His methods of selecting and bringing on promising young riders and horses and the success of his Interval Training programmes were proven beyond doubt when the United States won not only the team gold medal but also the individual gold and silver.

Britain, for so long at the top of the eventing tree, went down in a series of disasters that should not happen to a team in a year, let alone one day. During the cross-country phase two of their horses went lame and the rider of a third lost time through concussion caused by a fall. On the final show-jumping day, with only two horses fit to compete, Britain was unable to qualify as a team. Even had all four horses stayed sound they would have been defeated by the United States.

But the test of a three-day event depends on the severity of the course. The real story of Bromont begins in the mind of the course designer.

The course designed

In June 1974 Barbara Kemp, an administration officer in the out-patients' clinic at Montreal General Hospital, was asked to plan the course for the 1976 Olympic Games. Miss Kemp had been one of the first people in Canada to become interested in Eventing, her enthusiasm initially aroused by a visit to Badminton in 1951. Since then, starting in 1952, she had designed a course every year in Canada. She was therefore the most experienced Canadian course builder and the natural choice for the Montreal Olympics.

The site chosen for the Olympic Three-Day Event was Bromont, a ski resort area 53 miles east of Montreal. In August 1974 it was officially approved by the International Equestrian Federation.

Barbara Kemp's initial and unwavering idea was to build the course on the natural hill terrain as it was at Bromont, making no attempt to construct a park course that was not native to the landscape. She began by becoming thoroughly familiar with the ground, and by mid-October 1974 she had an idea of the site of every fence.

During the following winter she skied all round the course, confirming the best lines for roads and tracks as well as for the cross-country.

OPPOSITE: the poster for the Montreal Olympics.

With the hillsides covered by smooth drifts of snow, topographical features that had been obscured by the verdure of summer became more visible. An old loggers' trail, long overgrown, that followed the contour line through a forest now stood out clearly in the winter whiteness.

The cross-country line that was taking shape in Barbara Kemp's mind ran from a small stream valley up through virgin woodland along the logging trail. From there it went through a small housing estate, over a golf course, and back by a circuitous route through the valley. What she had chosen was the line that seemed to her the most suitable way of getting from one part of the country to another; also, considering the steep ski slopes of Bromont, a line that did not involve too much ascent or descent.

When Barbara Kemp had sorted out the main drift of her line she skied it again to find out factors that might affect some competitors unfairly; things, for instance, such as where the neighbourhood dogs ran out. She studied particular fence sites, remembering that every obstacle had to be readily accessible to emergency medical vehicles as well as to repair crews. Then she established the direction of the prevailing wind, arranging the finish of the course so that tired horses should be helped by the flow of air. She took every opportunity to study current European trends in course design, later attributing much to the advice of Frank Weldon.

'In building a course,' she said, 'the first consideration has got to be the horse. The second consideration must be the public, because if you have no spectacle you have no sport. If you correlate these two, a tired and exhausted horse will deter the public, and lack of ability to see the fences will spoil the sport. Therefore groups of fences help viewers and also give a horse a chance to catch its breath, a change of pace to get its second wind. One aspect of group fences that you should always consider is their crowd appeal.'

An Olympic course is the hardest of all event courses to design, since, though the strength of competition is controlled at national levels by qualifying contests and is often also known at local international meetings, rules ensuring the high standard of entrants do not apply to an Olympic meeting. Olympic horses and riders need only to be nominated by their countries of origin, and it does not necessarily follow that they have had previous experience of sophisticated event courses. Therefore the Olympic course designer must not only challenge the best in the world but must also make allowances for indifferent performers.

'At Bromont the shortest route was always the hardest one,' Barbara Kemp said. 'I tried to build the course so that a bad horse could jump a safer way round for more time faults. However, I had no guarantee that the rider of a less-good horse would have the sense to take the safe route.'

The rules governing an Olympic three-day event speed and endurance course include the following: no more than 50% of the fences may be of maximum height, and there may be no more than

Barbara Kemp.

OVERLEAF: A 'trappy' hill course making full use of the local country. The endurance test lay more in the nature of the terrain – the climbs and descents and the frequent twists and turns – than in the size of the fences, which were not exceptionally large.

two maximum drops. The numbers of obstacles consisting of several elements, or 'combinations' as they are more commonly known, may not exceed a ratio of 1:10; that is, on a cross-country containing 30–40 fences only three may be combinations. The length of the cross-country phase can be either 7410 metres (13 minutes), 7695 metres (13·30 minutes) or 7980 metres (14 minutes). The steeplechase course must be 3450 metres (5 minutes), 3795 metres (5·30 minutes) or 4140 metres (6 minutes). The total of roads and tracks, phases A and C combined, must be between 16 and 20 kilometres (10–12 miles).

The course Barbara Kemp finally chose at Bromont measured 6000 metres on Phase A, 3450 on Phase B, 10,320 on Phase C and 7695 on Phase D, a total of 27·465 km. The optimum time for this was 1 hour 26 minutes and 30 seconds, plus 10 minutes in the Box at the start of Phase D. She explained the unequal division of the roads and tracks and the short steeplechase time with these reasons: 'Phase A should be long enough to limber up all the horse's tendons and circulation, Phase B is only to prove that he can jump at this great speed, and Phase C should relax him after the steeplechase but should not be long enough to bore him.

Construction of the Bromont course began in October 1975. Despite the absence of qualified fence builders and the menace of continually disruptive political pressure, Barbara Kemp pioneered in building what proved to be a first-rate Olympic test.

Work was still not completed when the first teams, the far-flung Australians and the high-altitude Mexicans, arrived to get acclimatized.

Lull before the storm

Normally Bromont is hot and dry in summer. In July 1976 it was warmish and wet. Abundant wildflowers sprouted over the meadows and roadsides, and the clouds above the steep, tree-clad hills alternated from fat white puffballs to turbulent thunderheads. Three weeks before the three-day event was due to start the Mexican and Australian horses standing in the new, red-painted stable blocks were plunged hock-deep in water because of a cloudburst.

The equestrian athletes – the three-day eventers, showjumpers and dressage teams – were housed together half a mile from the stable block in an overcrowded unit, called the Olympic Village for the duration of the Games (subsequently it was called low-cost housing, which was the purpose behind its original construction). A high mesh fence surrounded the 400-flat block, there were electronic checks on everyone who went in and out, and 700 police lay up in the wilderness around the Village or openly lounged with carbines against the perimeter of the fence. Because of the murder of the Israeli athletes at the Munich Olympics and the aftermath of world-wide political assassinations and kidnappings, security at Bromont was exceptional.

Security in the stable blocks was just as strict. The stables, which were beautifully constructed of wood, were numbered and labelled with each country's name on the outside. Each block housed tack

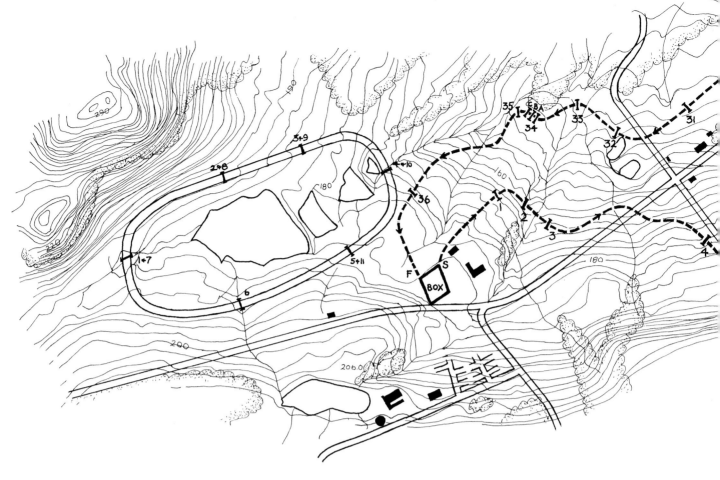

CONTOUR MAP OF
OLYMPIC CROSS-COUNTRY COURSE
Bromont 1976

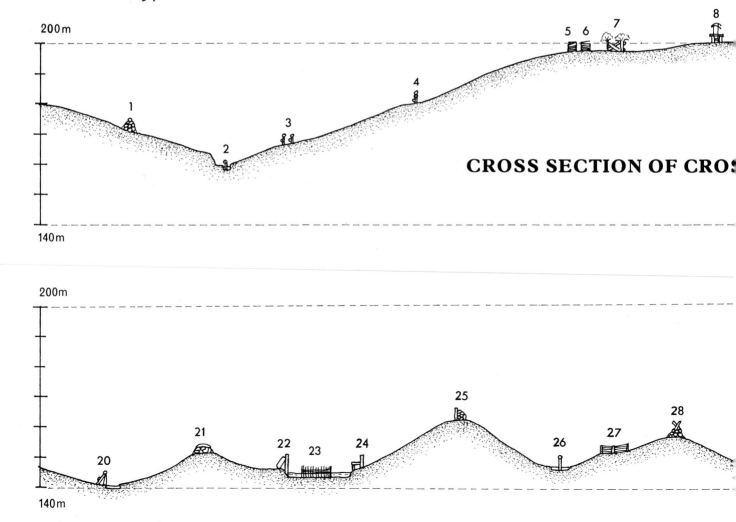

CROSS SECTION OF CROS

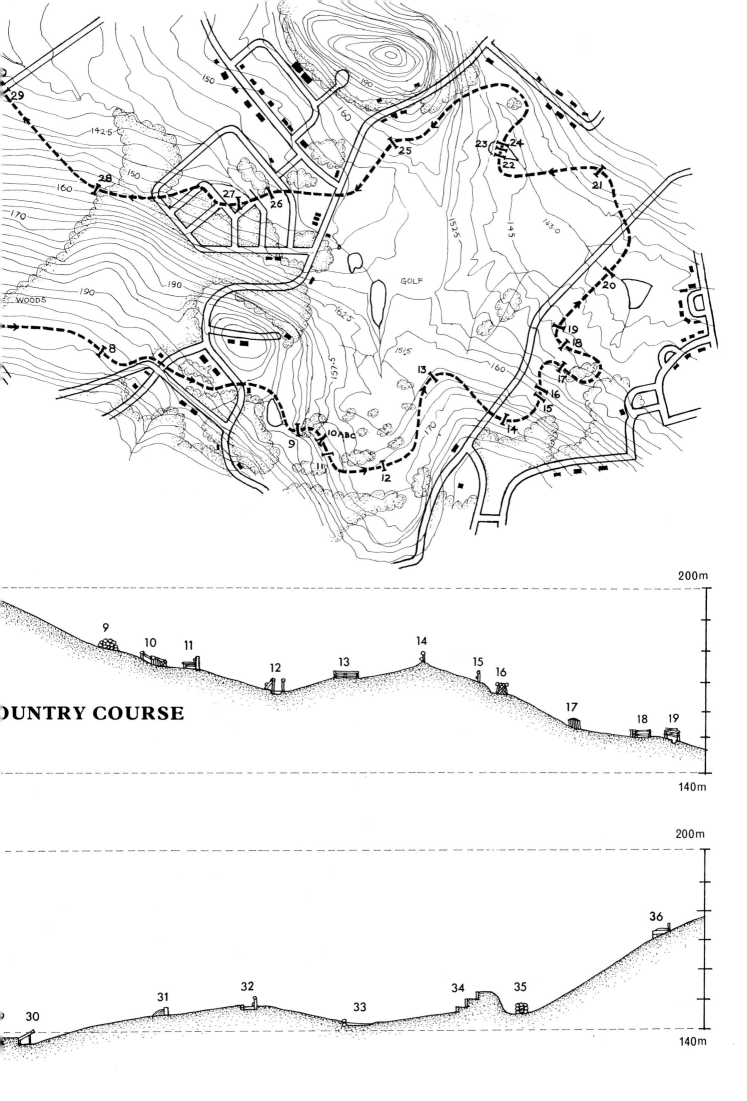

COUNTRY COURSE

Bill Roycroft of Australia,
at 61 the oldest competitor.

rooms, feed rooms, a bed for a groom on overnight duty, and refinements such as refrigerators stocked with soft drinks. There was an atmosphere of efficient calm.

On the hillside above the stables every type of cross-country fence was available for practice. Seventeen dressage and showjumping practice arenas, splattered throughout the area, were of exceptional standard – most top three-day events have not even one sanded arena. The groom's quarters, too, were unparalleled (Wilma Lusty, groom to the Dutch showjumping team, described them as 'the grooms' Hilton'). The only noticeable defect was that the new-laid turf around the stable block had been sprayed, to make it grow faster, with a chemical that, unfortunately, was poisonous to horses.

In the week or two before the three-day event began on 22 July, teams from all over the world flew in to get their horses settled into the new environment. Germany came, and Russia, the USA, Italy, Great Britain, Ireland, Australia, France, Argentina, Mexico, Japan, Italy, Guatemala, and, of course, the home team, Canada. Each team wore its own country's track suit, starting practice – sometimes as early as 6 am, according to the daily rota of work hours allotted by the stable manager – in the immaculate sanded arenas, which were raked after each use by tractors, or merely exercising along the abundant hill trails of Bromont. The variety of trails was such that you could ride for two hours without crossing your own tracks and still be in the security area, and because of this the intelligent three-day event horses settled easily and happily into their surroundings.

Passing time from day to day before an event of such international importance can be disturbing. Animators (sic) were provided for the teams, 14 for the competitors and eight for the grooms. Their jobs, literally, were to animate anyone who seemed lonely, bored or ill-adjusted. These animators were college students specializing in sport. They had been trained to be sympathetic, and were officially told not to eat onions or garlic.

Competitors who were lucky enough to take trips into the Montreal Village may have been diverted by the notice on the door of the Irish Delegation, which read, 'These offices are open from 8.00 to 18.00 hours, except for the times when they are closed.' Or by the Russian Delegation's red-flagged headquarters, with its large portrait of Lenin looking down on the crowd. 'Look, there's Lenin!' a passing English journalist said, taken aback. 'Great god,' responded an American reporter, 'maybe our lot should put up a portrait of Nixon.'

In the final few days before the Briefing of Competitors on 21 July life at Bromont took on an added edge, possibly because the official opening ceremony of the Games, held four days earlier in Montreal, had made everyone realise just what was about to happen. The constant visual shock of high-quality horseflesh was also a reminder that this was to be no run-of-the-mill event.

Yet some of the horses, disappointingly, were not at their best. Ut Majeur, a kind-eyed French horse thin as a grasshopper because of a virus he had contracted before leaving France, made visible daily progress on a lead-rein around and in the lake where the competitors and grooms swam but never appeared to carry more muscle than a battery hen. Cambridge Blue, one of the best of the Irish horses, lamed himself through an unfortunate landing in a bog over a practice water jump and did not recover in time for the competition.

In the United States stables the horses had it as soft as millionaires on a health farm. All of them got *shiatsu*, the Japanese pressure points massage, from a professional sports masseur named John Meagher. 'I've been working with humans for thirty years, and there's nothing in a horse you won't find in a man,' Meagher said. He was a powerfully-built person with a good-humoured face. 'When you massage human athletes they tell you they are better in consequence because they know they should be. But, of course, it's different with a horse.

'They're the biggest, toughest, strongest horses in the world, these three-day event horses. They're the greatest athletes on earth: what athlete could do more than an eventer?' Here he dug his fingers into a sensitive point on Irish Cap, the charming, conceited World Champion who had nearly died of a lung complaint in 1975. *Shiatsu* can be painful. Irish Cap, disapproving, coughed with displeasure. He had learned during his lung illness that coughing brought him sympathy, and did it now for effect—the only horse at Bromont who could cough without raising a panic in the stables.

Close by, in the gangway that ran down the centre of the stable block, Marcus Aurelius, Mary Anne Tauskey's 15.1 h h narrow bay mount, stood on a lead-rein to be groomed. His nickname was 'the Bionic Pony', a label derived from the freakish strength of the hero of the American television programme *Six-Million Dollar Man*. Marcus Aurelius had warts on his nose. In the stable beside him Bally Cor, the only mare on the team and, ridden by Tad Coffin, the winner of the 1975 Pan-American Games, stretched out on her side, asleep.

Sitting on the poisoned turf outside the USA stable block, Bruce Davidson finished up a sunny interview with a non-equestrian reporter: '. . . You're not just travelling with yourself and your own uniform but with your horse and his. I think I can modestly say it's an expensive sport....

'Why do I do it? – You're obviously not a horseman! I do it for *him* (Irish Cap). I broke him, I trained him, I brought him on.

'My brother's a golfer. I think golf's a boring sport, but my brother walks a golf course the way I walk a cross-country course. It becomes an art form.'

The worst pressures may have been on the British, who had won the team gold at the last two Olympics and who were expected to win again. Being favourite is a heavy responsibility.

Under way

On Wednesday 21 July, the day began officially with one of the most articulate and helpful briefings of competitors that had ever been given. The 'briefer' was the father of Juliet Graham of the Canadian team. From then on the course was open to inspection.

A dressage test nears its end, the movements of the competitor recorded on the freshly-raked sand.

During the rest of the day, before the 4 pm veterinary inspection, competitors straggled out nervously to see what Barbara Kemp had let them in for. Many looked concerned, but the Australian team, least-subsidized of any team competing, treated the taxing course with humour. Inspecting the jump out over fence 30, the punishing Cat's Tomb drop after the second crossing of the main Gaspé road that ran through the valley, an observer congratulated team captain Bill Roycroft on his courage. 'We're not brave,' Roycroft responded cheerfully; '—we're just silly.'

Bill Roycroft, competing in his fifth Olympic three-day event, was then 61 years old. He had won more three-day events than anyone else in the world, including the team gold medal at the Rome Olympics despite a collar bone broken during the performance. At Munich he had carried the Olympic banner for Australia with a broken toe. His son, Wayne, was also on the event team, and another son, Barry, was competing for Australia as a showjumper.

All the Australians knew that they would have to sell their horses after the competition because Australia's mandatory six-month quarantine period in England before being allowed back home would cost more than they could afford. Their only event horse who would see his homeland again was Hillstead, a 16-year-old belonging to Sydney newsagent Denis Piggott. Hillstead's quarantine fees had been raised by subscription in the village where he lived.

Other participants saw problems that did not exist. At the Duck Blind, centre fence of the three that stood in and around the lake, four convincing decoy ducks had been added for ornament. One of the team trainers, thinking they were real, waded in and tried to scare them into flight.

The late afternoon veterinary inspection produced the horses in public for the first time. One by one the most famous names in the world were trotted up, examined by the panel, and passed fit to compete. There was applause for the striking, high-actioned trot of Germany's Albrant, and laughter for the two proud Mexican stallions who reared and showed off before the crowd. The most unusual horse was one of the fine but seldom-seen Russian breeds, probably a Budyonny, which had a metallic golden sheen on its bay coat.

That evening the teams were announced, with some surprises coming among the nominated horses. Jack Le Goff, grand master of the American team, had opted for his younger horses instead of the more experienced veterans such as World silver medallist Good Mixture. Le Goff's selections had much to do with the questionable soundness of the older horses on ground more taxing than a park course, but he explained that his choice had also to do with the trappy nature of Bromont, reasoning that an experienced and bold horse who was making his own decisions would get into more trouble than a horse who was still listening to his rider.

Thursday started coolly, without fanfare or announcement. The dressage competition began with the usual trial rider, performing the test so that the judges could get their eye in before they began marking anyone. The crowd, believing this to be the first competitor, applauded.

As the morning drew on, Friday's competitors warmed up in the practice arena behind the collecting ring, getting their horses used to the atmosphere of crowds and flags and tension. Some rode openly through the throngs in the public area.

In the afternoon, rapt silence marked the test of Princess Anne, broken only by cameras whirring like a battery of dragonflies. Goodwill, jumping out of his skin with vitality, broke twice from a trot into a canter, ending midway down the list with a penalty score of 91·25. When they left the arena half the crowd went home.

On Friday the third and fourth members of each team performed their tests. Viktor Kalinin on Araks, best of the Russian squad at dressage, rode in the distinctive Russian style with his arms often straight from shoulders to fingers. Araks was totally obedient, giving to his rider with a visible desire to please; yet 85·84 penalties was all they could achieve.

Great gusts of wind buffeted the crowd surrounding the sheltered arena. Good theatre came from Bill Roycroft, maximizing his shock of white hair with a shining black topper, a scarlet tailcoat and a grin; and from Lucinda Prior-Palmer, who trotted round the outside of the arena waiting for the judges' call to start her test on a loose rein, more as if out for a hack than in for a contest, and then performed gaily and accurately with a smile for the crowd.

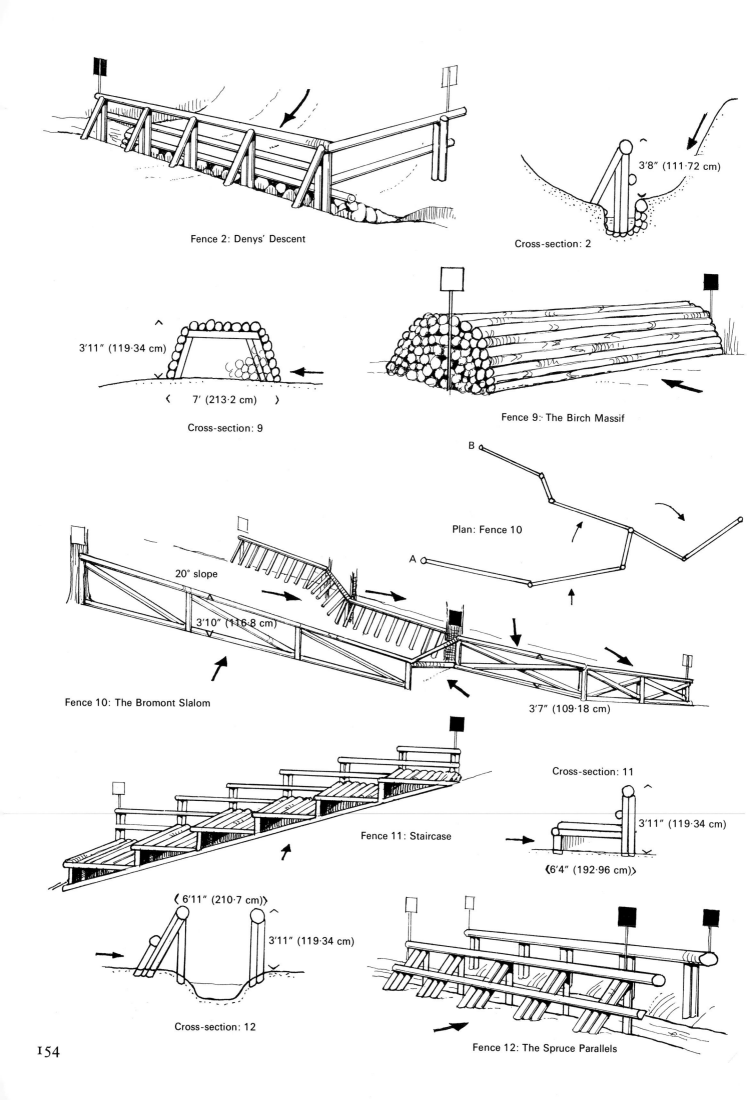

Fence 2: Denys' Descent

Cross-section: 2

3'8" (111·72 cm)

3'11" (119·34 cm)

7' (213·2 cm)

Cross-section: 9

Fence 9: The Birch Massif

Plan: Fence 10

B

A

20° slope

3'10" (116·8 cm)

Fence 10: The Bromont Slalom

3'7" (109·18 cm)

Cross-section: 11

Fence 11: Staircase

3'11" (119·34 cm)

《6'4" (192·96 cm)》

《6'11" (210·7 cm)》

3'11" (119·34 cm)

Cross-section: 12

Fence 12: The Spruce Parallels

154

OPPOSITE AND OVERLEAF:
Some of the fences from
the cross-country course.
The plan of fence 10 shows
the normal path of
approach, although the
fence could also be
taken from the right
hand side.

But neither of these was good enough to match the statuesque control of Bruce Davidson and Irish Cap, or the outstanding symmetry of Germany's Karl Schultz and Madrigal, who gave easily the best performance of the competition.

At the end of Friday the individual placings were 1. Karl Schultz, with 46·25 penalty points; 2. Bruce Davidson (54·16); 3. Germany's Otto Ammermann on Volturno (58·7); 4. Canada's Jim Day on Viceroy (60·00); 5. Lucinda Prior-Palmer (62·91); 6. Tad Coffin on Bally Cor (64·59); 7. Mike Plumb on Better and Better (66·25). Overall, Germany led from the United States team, with Britain in third place.

These results were almost exactly as expected. The best event horses in the world had consistently performed the best dressage tests. Disappointingly, though, there had also been a large number of very inadequate tests for an Olympic Games. Karl Schultz's excellent performance had been taken for granted long before the competition began, and everyone had thought that Bruce Davidson would be the one to finish behind him. The only slight turn up had been Jim Day's good score, a surprise because his horse was comparatively new to eventing and was not known on the international scene.

An unusual feature of the dressage marking was that it had a multiplying factor of 1·25. Normally the multiplying factor is 1, meaning that the number of penalties incurred by each rider stands as his final score. Scores at Bromont were expressed as one-and-a-quarter times the total penalties (probably because the cross-country was expected to sort the riders out more widely than it normally does); thus the dressage totals were spread over a wider range of marks and advantages gained in dressage were of more than usual importance.

With the cross-country ground drying out well under a warm wind, the value of the dressage advantage was more than ever emphasized. Yet, though many observers still believed that the cross-country course would prove too easy, those with real knowledge talked about it with respect.

'It's a very tough course,' said General Prior-Palmer, who had ridden in the exhausting Indian Army trials at Saugor in the 'thirties and so knew a lot about endurance. 'That hill at the beginning: you have to decide whether to push on to get the time and risk tiring your horse, or save him here and get time penalties. It's all hook and push, hook and push.'

Major Derek Allhusen, himself a veteran Olympic rider, was also worried. 'The course is much more punishing than you think,' he said. 'The one thing that exhausts a horse is losing impulsion on an uphill turn and then having to go on up again.' He had doubts, too, about the steeplechase course. 'We're unused to galloping on sand. It'll take much more out of the horses than we expect.'

The test anticipated
The cross-country course was gravelly and often uneven. Changes of altitude were the biggest problem. From fence 2 to fence 4 the land

climbed 125 feet, dropping 100 feet from the ninth to the twelfth and rising sharply another 125 feet from the lake (fences 22–24) to the ornamental posts and rails of fence 25, the Olympic Garden.

Bogey fences did not turn out always as expected. Fence 2, a steep bank dropping to a narrow stream with a post and rails built over it, gave nothing like the trouble that the crowd round it suggested it should; while number eight, the Sleigh-Ride Bar, a canopied table coming unexpectedly on an uphill turn along the logging trail, stopped eight horses in their tracks.

The fence that caused most upset was a brute of ingenuity – fence 10, the Bromont Slalom, a three-part nasty constructed on a 180-degree turn on a 20-degree downhill slope on the golf course. There was no way that the Slalom, with its additional problems of trees standing between the fences and a precipice falling away beyond the second and third elements, could be negotiated without pulling the horses back to a hand canter. One of Barbara Kemp's objectives in building it, apart from the test of horsemanship, had been to break the galloping pattern of the horses and give them a chance to catch their breath.

Fence 11, the Golfers' Staircase yards away across the steep slope of the fairway, was to trouble no one seriously. But silly accidents can happen in eventing even to the most experienced. Here, Germany's Herbert Blocker and Albrant lost a stirrup leather when the safety catch slipped. Blocker jumped the remaining 25 fence with only one iron, finishing with such severe cramp that he had to be lifted off his horse.

Debbie's Dilemma, a big, multi-angled post and rails on to a downhill landing, accounted for six competitors. Two showed heroism worthy of the toughest of the early Military tests: Van der Vater of Ireland cracked three ribs here and fractured a shoulder blade, yet went on to the finish despite a refusal at the water; and Germany's Helmut Reitemeier, disabled when his mare Pauline fell on top of him, got up ashen-faced and completed the course; he also had three cracked ribs.

One of the best fences for the onlooker was, predictably, the water (fences 22–24). It lay in a natural amphitheatre on the golf course. There was a 3′ 8″ jump in over a pair of boats laid end to end, a centre jump in the lake over a brush-laced post and rails named the Duck Blind, and a heave out on a shallow bank topped by Bobby's Benches, a rustic seat affair. Eight horses fell or were eliminated in the water.

For those who had survived that far the rest may have seemed comparatively plain sailing. On a fresh horse much of it could have been easy; but horses nearing the end of an Olympic speed and endurance test need help, and riders, mentally taxed and physically tired, are prone to errors that in cold blood might seem stupid.

The final three fences were a demonstration of tactical ingenuity. Fence 34, Dunlavey's Banks, consisted of three sleeper-faced upward leaps which demanded speed and strength from a tired horse. 'The knowledge of the Banks kept the riders back earlier in the course,' Barbara Kemp explained. 'Everyone knew that they just had to hold a

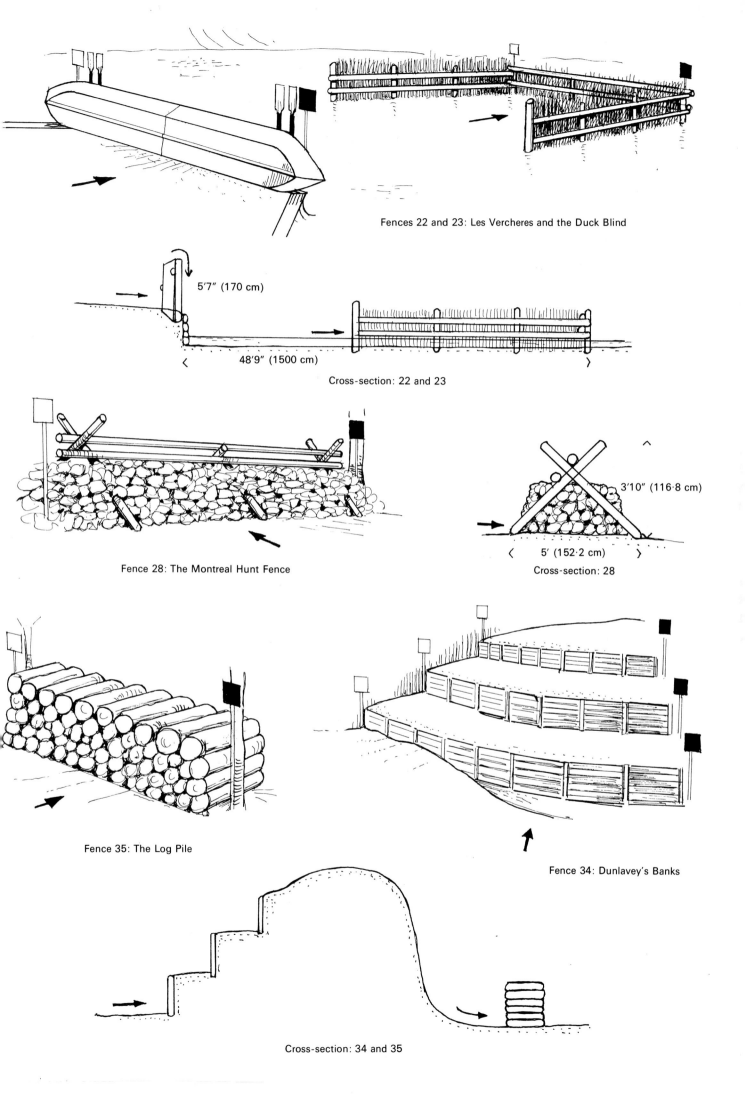

Fences 22 and 23: Les Vercheres and the Duck Blind

5'7" (170 cm)

48'9" (1500 cm)

Cross-section: 22 and 23

Fence 28: The Montreal Hunt Fence

3'10" (116·8 cm)

5' (152·2 cm)

Cross-section: 28

Fence 35: The Log Pile

Fence 34: Dunlavey's Banks

Cross-section: 34 and 35

horse together at the Banks. Without this knowledge there would have been faster times.'

Going straight over the top of the tree-clad knoll above the banks the path slid abruptly down into a log pile with only one awkward approach stride before the jump. The rest was a sweet run home on grass, a rewarding canter through, no doubt, a cheering crowd – but just before the finish came a puny little fence, the Mangers, only 3′ 2″ high and 4′ wide; a fence to foil anyone into careless riding. Canada's Cathy Wedge and City Fella, clear up to now, tripped over this one. The horse was winded.

Concours complete
In the early hours of Saturday morning, while it was still dark, a colossal thunderstorm burst on Bromont. It was still raining lightly at 8 am, when the first horse, the Mexican Cocaleco, ridden by Captain Mariano Bucio Ramirez, set off on the start of Phase A. Clouds blotted out the surrounding hilltops, and the white sunhats of the Olympic officials dripped limply on to plastic mackintoshes. 'I think,' said Michael Clayton, editor of the British magazine *Horse and Hound*, 'that this is where the British flat cap really comes into its own.'

Security was as strong as ever. Competitors not only underwent the usual checks for boots and spurs but also took their helmets off in case a walkie-talkie radio should be concealed. Each horse was dope-tested immediately after each performance of each day, urine samples

Captain Roberto Redon Tavera (Mexico) wanted to jump the Twin Trakeners. Arrupe didn't.

158

labelled and stored in a deep-freeze in case any question of foul play might arise. Some were later analysed on random selection.

Hugh Thomas and Playamar, the first to go for the British team, had an agonising ride reminiscent of Michael Moffatt's Badminton 1973 experience with Demerara. In 1975 Playamar had been successfully operated on for trouble with a deep flexor tendon on his off fore. Now, at the Bromont Slalom, he gave out again on the same leg, though this time with a superficial flexor tendon. Had he been riding as an individual, Hugh would have retired. As a team member he felt obliged to go ahead, falling into the lake but otherwise coming home clear. Later, Playamar was judged not sound enough to continue.

Others, too, had disappointing experiences. The Argentinian horse, Dos de Oro, fell over the Snake and the Duck Blind and retired. Germany's Otto Ammermann and Volturno, who had finished so strongly in the dressage, incredibly failed to go through the correct finish on the steeplechase and were later eliminated. Canada's Robin Hahn and L'Esprit fell at the birch rails at the bottom of the golf course, fell again at the lake, and went tiredly and gamely on to the finish.

The storm that had been loitering over the hilltops broke again on the next competitor, Princess Anne, who started in a blinding sheet of rain and fell at the 19th fence when Goodwill floundered unexpectedly in the take-off ground. Though he was winded and she concussed they went on again to a flawless finish, the rider guided by courage and will-power to complete the course. Precisely what had occurred – whether Goodwill actually fell on Princess Anne or not – was never established, as she remembered nothing from the approach to the fateful fence to the end of the course. In the subsequent enquiries about whether this horse-and-rider combination was included on the team because of the rider's royal birth the important points were disregarded: first, the combination of Princess Anne and Goodwill had, ten months earlier, won the European individual silver medal. Second, she was one of only two of the four members of her nation to complete the circuit.

The Japanese horse Inter Nihon, like the two other horses on his team, had no liking for the course. Falling over the Snake, he refused twice at the Hanging Elm and once at the Sleigh-Ride Bar. At the Slalom he stopped again and was lapped by the Guatemalan rider Rita de Luna on Pampa, who came gaily over the first part of the fence and refused the second element, where Pampa stopped so abruptly that he slid into the fence on his bottom.

Here a very serious accident could have occurred. Both Pampa's forelegs were stuck through the vee-shaped posts of the fence. Sitting squarely on his backside with no purchase for his hind legs in the wet earth, he could have broken a foreleg if he had panicked. Instead he sat calmly, unable to get out; while, incredibly, an official of the Canadian Equestrian Federation repeatedly kicked his bottom. The crowd around the Slalom became hysterical, screaming at the official to stop. Entirely due to his rider's self-possession Pampa was helped

Van der Vater (Ireland) and Blue Tom Tit. The rider has three cracked ribs and a cracked shoulder blade.

to find a purchase with his hind feet, and backed gently out of the dangerous situation.

Juliet Graham and Sumatra, riding a fine round for Canada with the best time of her team (81·6 penalties), went just ahead of Tad Coffin, riding in the American number two spot. Tad was a worry to his team because of his dependence on the drug neosynephrine for a permanent sinus condition. Olympic athletes are not allowed to take drugs, and the wet, humid Bromont weather was particularly hard for a man who could not breathe through his nose. Riding with his mouth open for air, Coffin went round in the fastest time so far – 50·5 penalties. The only person to beat that time, or even to approach it, was the magnificent American veteran Michael Plumb on the 7-year-old Better and Better, who clocked 49·6. Richard Meade and Jacob Jones, a vastly-improved eight-year-old shown off beyond his expected scope by one of the most brilliant riders in the world, was third fastest with 57·6.

Fourth fastest round the course were Lucinda Prior-Palmer and Be Fair, who at 13 was the most consistent horse in the competition and the favourite with the crowd. Excelling at every fence with the flair for which he was world-famous, Be Fair came over the last to tremendous applause. But another lesson had been learned from Bromont – the best cross-country horse in the world could only improve one place on his dressage score.

Then, a few yards from the finish, moving easily along on the grass, Be Fair slipped an Achilles tendon on his hock. He finished so lame that an ambulance was needed to take him back to the stables.*

Other turn-ups in form were to follow. Bruce Davidson and the consistent Irish Cap had an unexpected fall over the Duck Blind. Bill Roycroft and Version fell at one of the smaller fences, the Crooked Bottle. But the most surprising performance of the day came from Karl Schultz and Madrigal, who had not been expected to excel cross-country. They went clear with only 63·2 time penalties, so maintaining their lead at the end of the second day.

Team results at the end of Saturday showed America in the lead from Britain, Germany third, Italy fourth, Australia fifth, Russia sixth, Ireland seventh and Canada eighth. Mexico, France, Japan and Argentina had been eliminated as teams, and Guatemala, who had only entered two horses, had anyway never competed as a team.

Individual placing were now 1. Karl Schultz; 2. Tad Coffin; 3. Mike Plumb; 4. Lucinda Prior-Palmer; 5. Richard Meade, and 6. Italy's Giovanni Bossi.

It had rained all day during the speed and endurance test, the going becoming progressively deeper and the sand on the steeplechase riding dead and tiring. It seemed to have rained particularly hard on the British who, though in second place overall, were eliminated as a team because of the unsoundness of Be Fair and Playamar.

The conclusion drawn at this stage of the event was that dressage

*September 1976: Be Fair is making an excellent recovery. He has a pleasant future in the hunting field, but will not again be able to take part in an event.

160

BROMONT 1976
Gaspe Bank and Cat's Tomb

Robin Hahn (Canada) and L'Esprit

This sequence is a good example of a strong rider 'carrying' a tiring horse. Contact is well-maintained throughout, even during use of the whip over the final element.

1. A long way up for a tiring horse. L'Esprit takes a good look at it. Hahn is driving on hard.

2. The rider positions his weight to give his horse maximum assistance, and...

3. picks up his horse on landing. The contact is never lost.

4. Hahn uses every inch of the road crossing to get momentum for the coming fence.

5 and 6: Not convinced the horse will make it, the rider uses extra assistance from his whip.

BROMONT 1976
Les Vercheres and the Duck Blind

Tad Coffin (USA) and Bally Cor

Tad Coffin's comments:

I made a pretty wide turn into it, at a gallop, then set her up a little bit and sat quiet and let her get on with it. She's always a little bit aggressive. I kind of sit on her and play it a little cautious.

1 and 2: Over the first one I sat pretty good on her – too much; more than I would like. But that's my problem in cross-country – I tend to take the back seat a little. There's a line to how much you have to sit back that's necessary and how much that's more than necessary.

3 and 4: It was 45 feet between the first and second parts. Basically two canter strides, but she trotted a stride or two.

5: She landed in, and looked, and knew where she had to go.

7, 8, 9: Not a difficult jump out for my mare. She's very clever. She has just enough talent to make it – the rest she does with her head.

4

7

5

8

6

9

performances had become more important than ever. Britain had fielded a team on the basis of four horses that would go across country. Only one of these, Be Fair, was known to be capable of world-class dressage. Richard Meade's good showing with Jacob Jones, a new-comer, was an unexpected surprise.

The final day

Sunday morning shone on everyone but Giovanni Bossi, whose horse, Boston, trotted up so lame at the veterinary inspection that it was surprising that Bossi could have hoped to get him accepted. With the British out of it and now also the best of the Italians lamed the Australian team position strengthened. Wayne Roycroft, seventh after the cross-country, automatically moved up to fifth place.

There was no parade before the show jumping. Each competitor came in and departed without suspense, a short time interval allowed between them. Twelve fences stood in the sanded arena. On top of the last, a wall, geraniums flowered. None of the jumps was big or awkwardly-sited, but a careless touch of a pole could alter the placings.

If the normal electricity of horse pursuing horse was lacking the drama was real enough – it happened behind the scenes. The starting scores were so close that Karl Schultz knew he had to go clear to keep his lead (provided, that is, that Coffin and Plumb went clear) and that he had only two fences in hand over Richard Meade. Yet Schultz, the gold medal now so nearly his, was clearly worried whether Madrigal, a hopeless show jumper, could hold his own. Van der Vater, in appalling pain, tried hard to sit on Blue Tom Tit in the warm-up area behind the stands, but realised he was not fit enough to go. Helmut Reitemeir made it on to Pauline's back, his broken ribs so agonising that, though he jumped round with only two fences down, he was afterwards taken away by ambulance.

Of the individual favourites Tad and Bally Cor went first – a striking, grey-eyed blond young man on a small bay mare with a white star on her forehead. Economical, professional, they kept very close to the fences and ended with a clear round, so assuring themselves of the individual silver. But unless Karl Schultz made a mistake they could make no improvement towards the gold.

Then Jacob Jones put a toe on the groundline after the water. Ten penalties, and Richard could not advance his place. Better and Better splashed into the water but otherwise went clear, so that Mike Plumb was still ahead of Richard Meade.

And lastly Madrigal. Karl came in looking very cool and collected, his mount slightly overbent in the traditional German show jumping style, the horse's head turning from side to side as the rider suppled him up.

Madrigal jumped long and flat, rigid as a horse with a steel bar down its spine. A rail fell from the second oxer, then another from the double parallels of fence 11. Over the final wall he went, the geraniums setting off his chestnut coat, and out of the arena with two fences on the ground. Poor Karl Schultz – the great chance gone.

1. Overnight leader Karl
Schultz (centre) wears the
German team track suit.
Note the security passes
worn round spectators'
necks.

2. Sunday morning
veterinary inspection.
The Canadians are accepted
fit. City Fella is led up for
examination as Sumatra
(foreground) leaves the area.

I

2

1. Waiting for show jumping:
Richard Meade's number
comes up.
2. Mike Plumb and Better
and Better over the last
fence but one.
3. Jack Le Goff counsels
Bruce Davidson.

4. Overspill on the hillside. The competition attracted a capacity crowd.
5. Tad Coffin, individual gold medallist.
6. Princess Anne and Goodwill midway through their clear round.

5

6

Tad Coffin at home.

After a brief delay they announced the results. 'First, and Olympic champion, Edmund Coffin, United States. Second, John Plumb, United States. Third, Karl Schultz, Germany.' Richard Meade was fourth, Wayne Roycroft fifth, and Gerry Sinnott of Ireland sixth.

Team results were 1. United States; 2. Germany; 3. Australia, the only team to have had four clear rounds showjumping (Australian radio had reported two days before that this team was no good, and that it was a waste of time and money sending it to the Olympics); 4. Italy; 5. Russia; 6. Canada, and 7. Ireland.

Edmund 'Tad' Coffin became the first American in the history of eventing to win an Olympic gold medal and also, at 21, the youngest rider ever to do so. When it was over he took off his show-jumping cap and reinstated 'Philip Felt', his favourite slouch hat.

On Monday 2 August, he went home to South Strafford, Vermont. The village gave him a rapturous welcome.

Into the future

The lessons learned from the 1976 Olympic Games are inescapable and in many ways saddening. Much of the pure sport of eventing – the lark across country on the rider's own horse – has vanished for ever except at elementary levels. A world-class event rider must now devote himself full-time to the job. This, under the present amateur ruling which does not allow riders to be paid for anything connected with riding or horses, is impossible except for those who are either independently rich or who are prepared quietly to bend the rules.

If the rulings governing the earliest Olympic Games were still adhered to the future of such as Tad Coffin would now be assured. Financial security would be his for life, either through gifts from a grateful nation and/or by salaried political appointments that he would not necessarily have to work at to earn his money. 'As it is,' he says, 'I can't live off what I make. The only way open to me is to become a straight professional. Either that, or get a government subsidy–but I don't think there's any way the government would support me all the year round. Anyone who is going to be top in the United States is going to have to spend all his time riding.

'I would rather earn my living by teaching, by buying and selling horses, or by charging for boarding and schooling horses than by selling my name as an advertisement for saddles, but at present I am not allowed to do either. The United States Equestrian Team subsidy makes it easy on you financially by charging cheap rents and so on to trainees, and there are also tax incentives for owners to donate horses to the team. But as long as the American Horse Shows Association's strict amateur rules are enforced many of us must either break those rules or resign.'

Coffin's candid assessment of the problems facing event riders is neither an exception nor a surprise. The cost of all varieties of equestrian sports are now so high that the Olympic Committee may have the unenviable choice either of altering their amateur rulings (which, of necessity, are universally though unofficially known to be bent by the majority of top riders), or of making a farce of the Games by allowing only the trickle of genuine amateurs to compete.

Other facts revealed by the Games – most notably in the case of the British dethronement – are that teams can no longer expect to win internationally with horses that are not of all-round quality. Nor can they rely, unless exceptionally lucky, on producing four superb horse-and-rider combinations at only a few weeks' notice. Britain, following the American example, now needs to buy top quality young stock at five or six years old – an expensive investment, since there is no guarantee that a promising youngster will turn out to be world class. Until Britain is able to take a positive financial step such as subsidizing the purchase of young horses and paying for a trainer it will remain at a disadvantage.

A further important step, proven beyond question by Jack Le Goff's storming successes after six years of hard work, would be the selection and training of promising teenage riders who will provide an adequate range of talent from which to draw future Olympic teams.

All this, like most hindsight criticism, is easy to say. To make any effective use of the apparent lessons of the Games at least the following questions have to be raised:

1. Who is going to pay for a store of young horses, subsidize young riders and pay a trainer?

2. *What* trainer? Le Goff has undoubtedly shown himself to be a genius, but who else is there in whom current competitors would universally show sufficient trust?

The finest event riders in the world (the Americans aside) have earned their success through individual training methods. Most would find it unthinkable to alter their hard-proven ways on the say-so of some outsider. This difficulty, incidentally, has already occurred in the tragic confrontation of Jack Le Goff with most of the great American riders when he was first appointed as team trainer. It is significant that, of the four who made up the gold-medal-winning team, only one – Michael Plumb – was not a progeny of the trainer.

Conclusions should never be adamant. Because the 1976 eventing ball bounced in a different court there is no guarantee that advances in the pattern of eventing have reached an optimum solution. What has been learned is only part of a continuing education in a sport that is still, for an ever-increasing audience, the finest and bravest in the world.

Appendices

The information herein is approximate since no one method of training, feeding, etc., can apply to every horse and rider. What follows is a guideline to methods that have proved successful in international eventing. It should be interpreted by the reader according to the capabilities and needs of his own animal.

Whether to event

Considerations to bear in mind before taking up eventing are finance, time and physical fitness. An event horse costs upwards of £1000 per annum to keep, depending on how many other horses are stabled in the yard to share labour and equipment and whether other animals are kept at livery to subsidise overheads. It is not usually practicable, unless large sums of money are available, to keep one horse by itself; nor, if the rider is serious about competitive eventing, is it advisable to stake everything on the continuing soundness of only one animal.

Time investment for one horse should be estimated at half a day every day of the week; for several horses, assuming labour is employed, each horse can be cared for in less time to the rider.

It is important for the potential event rider to handle his horse/ horses himself in all aspects of their work and care. Unless he does this he will not have sufficient knowledge to judge his employees. It therefore follows that a novice rider will require several years of practical experience before he attains the standard needed to succeed in an event.

What sort of horse to buy

There is no absolute definition of a successful eventer. Best potentials indicate a horse that is four years old or younger, 7/8 thoroughbred, 16 hh and over, has class, guts, and natural balance.

Early ground work

YEAR I

Hunt lightly through first winter (age four to five).

Early spring participate hunter trials and riding club events.

If satisfied with above, one-day events (novice class) late spring season.

Turn away during summer.

Four or five novice events in autumn; about one every two weeks.

Rest two–three months. Turn away if satisfied with performance in autumn events; alternatively hunt lightly if inadequate performance in cross-country phase.

YEAR 2

Spring: start in novice events and upgrade to intermediate; aim at a three-day event (intermediate) end of season.
Turn away two months during summer.
Autumn: intermediate and possibly open intermediate three-day event if sufficiently mature.
Turn away end autumn season.

YEAR 3

Bring up twelve–fourteen weeks before first three-day event.
Compete in open intermediate and advanced classes spring and autumn, depending on maturity of horse.
Usual rest periods during summer and winter.

14-week training programme preceding three-day event

WORK

1 Bring up from grass.
2 Ride daily for two hours a day at walk for two weeks.
3 Ride and school two weeks.
4 Interval Training starts: work every fourth day beginning two minutes' working canter, $1\frac{1}{2}$ minutes' rest, 3 minutes' working canter building up to approximately 10 (3) 10 (3) 10 in final weeks of training.

FEED

Four feeds a day – 7am, 12 noon, 4pm, 7pm.
Mixture oats and nuts (when first up from grass low protein nuts, changing gradually to high protein as work increases).
Boiled feed (linseed, whole oats, barley) in bran mash twice weekly.
Vitamin supplements as recommended by veterinary surgeon.

Physical exercise for rider

Physical fitness is essential: skipping 200 times a day, squash, tennis, etc., are all excellent for wind. Riding, especially trotting and galloping with short stirrups, develops leg muscle. Exercises such as habitually running upstairs on toes help maintain muscles.

Entering an event

At start of year apply to governing body of eventing for registration forms for rider and horse. Always read instructions and rules. Select events, fill in and post entry forms as applicable.

Routine procedure during one-day event

On arrival, unbox horse and ride on loose rein until settled; then work/lunge.
Return animal to horsebox.

Still-life in a stableyard. Useful extras for an event
rider's equipment list are parents and a friend.
The dog is not very useful.

Walk cross-country and show jumping courses.
Change into formal clothing.
Ride horse in $\frac{1}{2}$–1 hour before dressage test.
Fit boots (if worn) before show jumping; boots and bandages before cross-country. After cross-country wash down with tepid water, scrape and towel, walk dry, check for cuts etc. Offer water with the chill off. Rug up and bandage, load into horse box (hay net and small feed).
Go home.

On arriving home after an event
Check horse trots up sound.
Return to stable.
Medicate if and as necessary.
Ensure warm and content.
Bran mash, hay and water.
Leave alone to rest for night.
Clean and groom more thoroughly following morning, after horse is well rested. Trot up again to check soundness. Turn out in field for an hour, weather permitting, otherwise walk to ease stiffness.

Equipment

HORSE
Grooming kit
Hoof oil
Jute rug
Underblankets
Roller and breastplate
Best rug
String vest
Stable bandages
Exercise bandages
Halter
Bridle(s)
Saddle(s)
Surcingle
Numnah
Breastplate
Studs
Front boots
Back boots
Overreach boots
Lunge rein and whip
Jumping whip
Dressage whip
Horsebox or trailer

RIDER
Boots
Spurs
Breeches (minimum 2 pairs)
Blue or black coat
Velvet riding cap
Top hat and tail coat (optional: commonly borrowed if occasion insists)
Crash hat and silk
Cross-country sweater
White hunting stocks
Stock pin
Cross-country gloves: string with rubber finger grips (leather slips when wet with sweat or water)
Gloves for dressage
Stop-watch

Glossary

Technical terms used in the book which may not be universally familiar:

Cannon bone: the main frontal bone of the leg between knee and fetlock or hock and fetlock. The hind cannon bone is sometimes erroneously called the 'shannon' bone, a name that originates not from medical distinction between fore and hind leg bones but from a printer's error in an army manual which appeared in the nineteen-fifties.

Cavaletti (sing. cavaletto): low rails used in the initial stages of teaching a young horse to jump. Each consists of a single rail attached at either end to an X-shaped support, which can be turned upside down to give the lowest height or on its side to give an interim height. Maximum height of the bar of a cavaletto is 19 inches, minimum height 10 inches, interim height 15 inches. The schooling jumps provided by cavaletti are used in the first instance to teach a horse to walk or trot over a rail. In subsequent lessons two or three cavaletti may be set up several paces apart, so that the horse learns to judge the length of his stride between obstacles; or two or more may be stacked on top of or beside each other so that the animal is initiated to jumps of varying heights and widths.

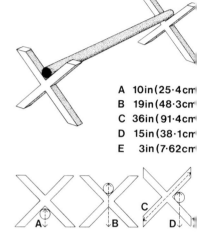

A 10in (25·4cm)
B 19in (48·3cm)
C 36in (91·4cm)
D 15in (38·1cm)
E 3in (7·62cm)

Counter canter: leading with the outside leg on a turn. At a canter or gallop the horse 'leads' with the same leg always in front, like a human skipping. Obviously it is easier for him to canter to the left with the left leg leading, and in normal circumstances he will automatically 'change legs' to suit the direction of his turn. A counter-canter to the left demands him to make the turn with the right leg in front, which requires obedience and good balance.

Deep going: the condition of the ground is described as 'going'. 'Good going' describes resilient ground on which the horse can move easily over the surface without sinking in, yet is not jarred by 'hard going' – i.e. bone-dry ground. 'Deep going' describes soft, wet ground into which the horse's hooves sink with every step, thus calling for extra exertion from the animal.

Drop fence: jump where the ground on the landing side is lower than on the take-off.

Gamgee: cottonwool-like substance used as a cushion under leg support bandages.

Hacking: riding at an undemanding pace, such as an easy walk, trot or canter as opposed to a 'working' trot or canter, in which the horse is required to use every muscle. Most recreational exercise, done on a loose rein, is 'hacking'.

Hand: the height of a horse taken from the withers (the highest point of a horse's back, just in front of the saddle) to the ground. Horses were originally measured not in feet and inches but in 'handbreadths' – the span of a man's hands placed one on top of the other. The average span of a hand being taken as four inches, 'hands' are now accepted as four-inch measures. Thus a horse that stands 16 hands high (commonly abbreviated as '16 hh') is 5′4″ tall from withers to ground. Hands are subdivided into four inches – thus 16.1 hh is 5′5″, 16.2 hh is 5′6″, 16.3 hh is 5′7″, 17 hh is 5′8″, and so on.

Hock: joint halfway down the hind leg of a horse; equivalent, since the horse stands on a toe in its hoof, to the human ankle.

Overreach: the long-striding hind foot strikes into the heel of the front foot, usually at a canter or gallop and most commonly in deep going. Since horses are shod with iron, this can cause a painful cut.

Peck: stumble on landing over a fence (when one or both forelegs trip or fail to land straight the horse's head goes down, rather like a chicken pecking corn).

Penalty area: pegged-out area surrounding each cross-country fence, inside which faults are penalized. Failure to keep within the penalty (or scoring) area at a fence or combination, as in making too wide a swing between separate elements, is also penalized. Falls outside the penalty area are not penalized.

Remuda: bunch of spare mounts herded along with a travelling cavalry or cowboy unit.

Spooking (slang): the cautious, erratic bound of a young horse over an unfamiliar obstacle, usually associated with the movement in which the animal takes an astonished look at whatever he is being asked to jump and shoots over it with an unnecessarily high leap out of the true line. A perfect example of spooking is illustrated on page 69.

Summer-holding ground: unlike 'winter-holding', in which the going is deep but wet through and so easier to slosh into and out of, 'summer-holding' ground often has a dried-out surface covering a plasticine-like subsurface. It is extremely tiring to gallop through.

Sweat rug: horse blanket akin to a human string vest, which keeps a damp horse warm while allowing water to evaporate through the air holes.

Tendon boots: leather support for the tendons, which lie behind the cannon bones, equivalent to ankle or wrist supports in humans.

Index

Page references to black-and-white illustrations are in *italic* type and to coloured illustrations in **bold** type.

Albrant, 153, 156
Albrighton Woodland Pony Club, 16
Allhusen, Maj. Derek, 155
Ammermann, Otto, 155, 159
Anne, HRH Princess, 35, **47**, *48*, 51, *92–3*, *98–9*, *114*, **138–9**, 153, 159, *167*
Araks, 153
Arrupe, *158*
Arthur of Troy, 99
Ayer, Mrs Frederick, 52
Ayer, Neil, 52

Baccarat, 39
Bally Cor, 151, 155, 164
Bayliss, Rachel, *34*, *132–3*
Beaufort, Duke of, 12, 15, 21
Be Brave, *68–9*
Be Fair, **30–1**, 34, *36–7*, **47**, *50–1*, 65, 67, 74, *76–7*, **130–1**, 160
Benson, 54
Better and Better, 62-3, 155, 160, 164, *166*
Bewas, River, 21
Blixen-Finecke, Capt. H. von, 22
Blocker, Herbert, 54, 156
Blue Tom Tit, *159*, 164
Bonanza's Little Dandy, *62*
Bossi, Giovanni, 160, 164
Boston, 164
Brazil, 108

Cambridge Blue, 151
Chalan, 40
Championnat du Cheval d'Armes, 20, 56, 59
Checcoli, M., 22
Chevallier, Capt. B., 21
City Fella, *165*
Clayton, Michael, 158
Cocaleco, 158
Coffin, Edmund ('Tad'), 151, 155, 160, 164, *167*, 168
Coleman, David, 35
Collins, Chris, *80–1*
Columbus, 44, *103*
Cornishman V, 40
Cotswold Vale Pony Club, 17

Davidson, Bruce, **41**, 44, *45*, 52, *53*, 54, *55*, 56, *57*, *58*, 59, 60–1, *63*, *102*, *142–3*, 151, 155, 160, *166*
Day, Jim, 155
'Dead Cert' (film), 40
Demerara, *11–17*, *134–5*, 159

Desourdy, Robert, **120–1**
Dos de Oro, 159

Edinburgh, HRH the Duke of, **41**
Evdokimov, Alexander, 39

Favour, *86–7*
Fédération Equestre Internationale, 40
Francis, Dick, 40
Furtive, *54*

George, **120–1**
Giles, Carl, *33*
Goff, Jack Le, 44, *58*, *59–61*, 63, 145, 153, *166*
Golden Griffin, *53*, 54, *63*
Good Mixture, 62, 153
Goodwill, 35, *48*, 99, **138–9**, 153, 159
Gordon-Watson, Mary, 40, *42*, *124–5*
Graham, Juliet, *43*, 151, 160
Gretna Green, *116–7*
Gurgle the Greek, *34*, *132–3*
Guyon, Adj. Jean-Jacques, 22, 59

Hammond, Barbara, *109*
Hannum, Carol, 59
Harley, **46–7**
Hatherly, Susan, 44, **46–7**, 51, 54, *126–7*
Hahn, Robin, 159, *161*
Highness, *124–5*
Hillstead, 152
Hodgson, Janet, 39, *47*, *50–1*, *114*, *116–7*
Hodgson, Maj. Peter, 42
Horse and Hound, 158

Indian Army School of Equitation, 21
Inter Nihon, 159
Interval Training, 40, 45, 60–1
Irish Cap, **41**, 44, *45*, *57*, 63, *102*, *142–3*, 151, 155, 160
Irwin, Cindy, *62*

Jacob Jones, 97, *102*, **122–3**, 160, 164
Jeger, 39

Kalinin, Victor, 153
Karsten, Horst, *43*
Kastenman, Sgt P., 22
Kemp, Barbara, 145, 146, *147*, 152, 156

Kilbarry, *29*
Kingmaker, The, 22, **24–7**

Laniugin, V., *103*
Larkspur, 39, *114*
Laureate, 54
L'Esprit, 159, *161*
Lithgow, Col Bill, 76
Luna, Rita de, 159
Lusty, Wilma, 150
Lynch, Maj. John, 58

Madrigal, 155, 160, 164
Marcus Aurelius, 151
Mardi Gras, *92–3*, *114*
Maribou, *126–7*
Meade, Richard, 22, 44, 97, *102*, **122–3**, **136–7**, 160, 164, *166*
Meagher, John, 151
Miller, Maj., 23
Moffett, Michael, *10*, *11–17*, 91, *134–5*, 159
Mohammed, 18–20
Mon Clos, 59
Moratorio, Capt., 40
Morgan, L., 22
Mörner, Count H., 21
Morthanges, Lt Ch. Pahud de, 21

Naylor-Leyland, Michael, *42*
Newton, Richard, 52
Nurmi, 20

Olivia, *82–3*
Olympic Games, 20–2, 145–69;
poster, *144*;
Bromont course, *148–9*
Omar Pasha, 18
Osberton, 74, 76

Paddy, 59
Pampa, 159
Pattinson, Aly, *82–3*
Pauline, 156, 164
Perkins, Beth, *54*
Persian Holiday, **130–1**
Phillips, Capt. Mark, 44, 84, *86–7*, *98–9*, 103, *108*, **130–1**
Pickles, 14
Piggott, Denis, 152
Pitou, 59
Plain Sailing, 44, 61
Playamar, 159
Plumb, Michael, *62–3*, 155, 160, 164, *166*
Prior-Palmer, Lucinda, 9, **30–1**, 34, *36–7*, **47**, 51, 61,

65, *68–9*, *73*, 74, *75*, 84, 97, *118–9*, **130–1**, 153, 155, 160
Prior-Palmer, Maj.-Gen. G.E., 155

Ramirez, Capt. Mariano Bucio, 158
Red Rusky, *109*
Red's Door, *62*
Reitemeier, 156, 164
Revere, Paul, 18
Rosen, Count Clarence von, 2
Royal Cor, 54
Roycroft, Barry, 152
Roycroft, Bill, *150*, 152–3
Roycroft, Wayne, 164
Russell, Lady Hugh, 9
Russell, Lord Hugh, 42, 63
Russo-Turkish war 1878, 18

Schultz, Karl, 155, 160, 164, *165*
Shedden, John, *91*
Sioux, *43*
'Six-Million Dollar Man' (TV Series), 151
Smokey VI, *80–1*
Stainless Steel, *88–9*
Stella, 23
Straker, Matthew, *120–1*
Stubbendorf, Capt. L., 21
Sumatra, *43*, 160

Tauskey, Mary Anne, 151
Tavera, Capt. Roberto Redon *158*
Thomas, Hugh, 159
Tommy Buck, *136–7*
Tost, *103*
Thorne, Diana, 22, **24–7**

Ut Majeur, 150

Vater, Van der, *159*
Vanier, *62*
Version, 160
Viceroy, 155
Vischy, Stefan von, 58
Volturno, 155, 159

Watkins, Torrance, *62*
Wedge, Cathy, 158
Weldon, Lt.-Col Frank, 12, 22, *29*, 32, 146
West, Debbie, 39, *78*
Wide Awake, 97, *118–9*
Wilson, Rowland B., *19*
Winter, Joanna, *88–9*

Xenophon, 18

Zijp, Lt A. vd V. van, 21